Money and the Middle Ages

Money and the Middle Ages

An Essay in Historical Anthropology

Jacques Le Goff

Translated by Jean Birrell

polity

First published in French as *Le Moyen Age et l'argent* © Perrin, 2010

This English edition © Polity Press, 2012

INSTITUT
FRANÇAIS

This book is supported by the Institut français as part of the Burgess programme.
(www.frenchbooknews.com).

Polity Press
65 Bridge Street
Cambridge CB2 1UR, UK

Polity Press
350 Main Street
Malden, MA 02148, USA

ISBN-13: 978-0-7456-5298-6
ISBN-13: 978-0-7456-5299-3(pb)

A catalogue record for this book is available from the British Library.

Typeset in 11 on 13 pt Sabon
by Toppan Best-set Premedia Limited
Printed and bound in Great Britain by MPG Books Group Limited, Bodmin, Cornwall

For further information on Polity, visit our website: www.politybooks.com

Contents

Acknowledgements

I would like to begin by expressing my gratitude to two people who have greatly helped me in writing this book. The first is that fine historian Laurent Theis, who suggested the subject and thus asked me to write the book you are about to read. He not only took this initiative, but he has given me constant support and made his own contribution by compiling the bibliography and by his careful reading and improvement of my text. The second person to whom I owe a special debt is my secretary and friend, Christine Bonnefoy, not only for her great technical skill but also for having engaged in a genuine dialogue with me as I dictated the text. Her fine intelligence helped me to see where revisions and improvements were needed.

I would like also to thank those colleagues and friends who have assisted me, in particular by allowing me to consult still unpublished work that was important for my subject. I will name the three to whom my debt is greatest: Nichole Bériou, Jérôme Baschet and Julien Demade. I also thank Jean-Yves Grenier, to whom I presented my project and who made a number of helpful observations.

In writing this book, I have given substance to ideas which already interested me when I published my first work. In a way, it completes my reflection on a subject I believe to be crucial for an understanding of the medieval period, in particular because the outlook and practices of the men and women of that age were so very different from our own. It is truly another Middle Ages that I have once again encountered.

Introduction

More than one word was used in the Middle Ages for the money that is the subject of this book, in the vernacular languages and in Latin. In the sense in which we use the word today, money was a product of modernity. It was not a major player in the medieval period, from the economic, political, psychological or ethical point of view. The realities of what we today call 'money' were not the chief components of what was then regarded as wealth. It has been claimed by a Japanese medievalist that the rich man was born in the Middle Ages, which is arguable; inasmuch as it is true, however, this rich man was as rich or richer in land, men and power than he was in cash.

As far as money is concerned, the Middle Ages was, in the *longue durée* of history, a regressive phase. Money was less important and less present than it had been in the Roman Empire, and certainly much less important than it would be from the sixteenth century, and even more the eighteenth century, on. Money was a reality which medieval society increasingly found it had to contend with, and it was beginning to assume the features that would characterize it in the modern period. Nevertheless, the men of the Middle Ages, including the merchants, the clergy and the theologians, never had a clear and unified conception of what we mean by this word today.

My book has two main themes. First, what was the role of money, or rather of coin, in the medieval economy, in medieval life and in medieval *mentalités*? Second, in a society dominated by religion, how did Christianity regard money and how did it teach Christians what attitude they should adopt to it and to the uses to which it could be put? On the first point, it seems to me that money never ceased to be rare and, most importantly, highly fragmented and diverse in the Middle Ages, and that this fragmentation was one of the causes of the difficulty experienced in achieving economic lift-off. On the second point, I believe that the pursuit and the use of money both by individuals and by states was gradually justified and legitimized by the institution that inspired and governed them, the Church, despite the conditions it attached to this justification.

It remains for me to emphasize, with Albert Rigaudière,[1] how difficult it is to define money as it is generally understood today and as it is discussed in this book: 'Its definition always eludes those who try to provide one. Both fact and fiction, substance and function, object and means of conquest, value of refuge and of exclusion, motor and end of relations between individuals, money cannot be confined within a single whole, any more than it can be reduced to a single one of its components.' I will try to take account of this multiplicity of meanings and specify the sense in which I use the word at every stage of this book.

For a study of the role of money in the Middle Ages, at least two main periods need to be distinguished. In a first Middle Ages, let us say from Constantine to St Francis of Assisi, that is, roughly, from the fourth to the end of the twelfth century, money was in retreat and coin was dying out, before it began slowly to return. The primary social distinction was between *potentes* and *humiles*, that is, between the powerful and the weak. Later, from the beginning of the thirteenth century to the end of the fifteenth, it was the distinction between *dives* and *pauper*, that is, between rich and poor, which came to dominate. The economic revival, the growth of towns, the strengthening of royal power and the preaching of the Church, especially the mendicant orders, made it possible for money to take off, though without, in my view, crossing the threshold of capitalism. This same period also saw the growth of voluntary poverty and a greater emphasis on the poverty of Jesus.

I would like at this point to emphasize two aspects of the history of medieval money. First, alongside real moneys, the

Middle Ages had moneys of account, which meant that medieval society, at least in certain milieus, achieved a skill in the sphere of accounting that it lacked in economic practice. Leonardo Fibonacci was a Pisan, son of a customs official of the Republic of Pisa located at Bougie, in North Africa. In 1202, he wrote in Latin a *Liber Abaci* (*Book of the Abacus* – an ancient tablet for calculation which became in the tenth century a table with columns using Arabic numerals) which is remarkable for his introduction of that essential discovery for accounting, zero. Progress in this sphere continued throughout the Middle Ages in the West, culminating, in 1494, in the publication by Brother Luca Pacioli of the *Summa de arithmetica*, a veritable arithmetical and mathematical encyclopaedia for the use of merchants. At about the same time, a *Method of Reckoning* was published in Nuremberg in southern Germany.

Next, as the use of money was always subject to religious and ethical rules, it will be helpful to note here the texts to which the Church referred in order to judge and, as necessary, put right or condemn those who used it. These texts are all from the Bible, and those that had a particular impact in the medieval West came from the New rather than the Old Testament, with one exception. This was a sentence which had huge repercussions among Jews and Christians alike, verse 31.5 of the *Book of Ecclesiasticus* (or *Book of Sirach*), which says: 'He that loveth gold, shall scarcely escape sin.' We will see later how the Jews were led, in spite of themselves, to neglect this advice wholesale and how medieval Christianity, as it evolved, nuanced it without ever losing the fundamental pessimism regarding money that inspired it. I give below the New Testament texts which had the greatest impact on attitudes to money:

1. Matthew, 6.24: 'No man can serve two masters: for either he will hate the one, and love the other; or else he will hold to the one, and despise the other. Ye cannot serve God and mammon' (in late Judaism, Mammon referred to iniquitous wealth, especially in monetary form).
2. Matthew, 19.23–24: 'Then Jesus said unto his disciples, Verily I say unto you, That a rich man shall hardly enter into the kingdom of heaven. And again I say unto you, It is easier for a camel to go through the eye of a needle, than for a rich man

to enter into the kingdom of God.' (These same texts are also found in the Gospels of Mark (10.23–25) and Luke (18.24–25).)

3 A passage in Luke (12.13–22) condemns the accumulation of wealth, especially 12.15: 'for a man's life consisteth not in the abundance of the things which he possesseth'. Later (12.33) Jesus says to his disciples, 'Sell that ye have, and give alms.' And finally Luke (16.19–31) tells the story, constantly repeated in the Middle Ages, of the rich man and the beggar named Lazarus; the former went to hell, the latter was welcomed in paradise.

One can imagine the deep impression these texts made in the Middle Ages. We find expressed in them the essence of what would throughout this period be the economic and religious context for the use of money, even though new interpretations softened its rigour: condemnation of greed, a capital sin, praise of charity and, lastly, from the perspective of salvation, which was essential to medieval men and women, exaltation of the poor and the presentation of poverty as an ideal incarnated by Jesus.

I would like now to throw light on the history of money in the Middle Ages by drawing on the evidence of iconography. The medieval images in which money appears, often symbolically, are invariably pejorative; they aim to make a deep impression on everyone who saw them so as to instil a fear of money. The primary image is of a particularly striking episode in the story of Jesus, the representation of Judas receiving the thirty pieces of silver for which he sold his master to those who were about to crucify him. For example, in a famous twelfth-century manuscript with many illustrations, the *Hortus deliciarum*, one folio represents Judas receiving the silver of his betrayal with the following commentary: 'Judas is the worst of merchants who incarnates the usurers whom Jesus expelled from the Temple because they put their hope in riches and wanted money to triumph, rule and dominate, which is a travesty of the praises celebrating the kingdom of Christ on earth.'

The principal iconographical symbol of money in the Middle Ages was a purse round the neck of a rich man dragging him down to Hell. This fatal purse, full of silver, is represented on conspicuously sited sculptures, tympanums and capitals of churches. It is also found, of course, in the Inferno of Dante's *The Divine Comedy*:

> So I went by myself still farther along the extreme margin of that seventh circle, where the woeful people were seated. Their grief was bursting forth through their eyes; with their hands they defended themselves, now here, now there, sometimes from the flames, sometimes from the burning ground; not otherwise do the dogs in summer, now with muzzle, now with paw, when they are bitten by fleas, or flies, or gadflies. When I set my eyes on the faces of some of these on whom the grievous fire descends, I did not recognize any of them, but I perceived that from the neck of each hung a pouch, which had a certain colour and a certain device, and thereon each seems to feast his eyes. And when I came among them, looking about, I saw, upon a yellow purse, azure that had the form and bearing of a lion. Then, gazing further, I saw another, red as blood, display a goose whiter than butter. And one, who had his white wallet marked with an azure and gravid sow, said to me, 'What are you doing in this ditch? Now get you gone! And since you are still alive, know that my neighbor Vitaliano shall sit here at my left side. With these Florentines am I, a Paduan; often they din my ears, shouting, "Let the sovereign knight come who will bring the pouch with three goats!"' Then he twisted his mouth and stuck out his tongue, like an ox that licks its nose. And I, fearing lest a longer stay should anger him who had admonished me to stay but little, turned back from the weary souls.[2]

1

The Heritage of the Roman Empire and Christianization

Christianity inherited from the Roman Empire a limited but significant usage of money, which then steadily declined from the fourth to the seventh century. In a famous but contested thesis, the great Belgian historian Henri Pirenne (1862–1935) argued that the appearance of Islam in the seventh century, and its conquest of North Africa and then Spain, put a stop to Mediterranean trade and economic exchanges between the West and the East. Without going to the other extreme, and accepting wholesale the contrary thesis of Maurice Lombard (d. 1964), who saw the Muslim conquest as a stimulus to the revival of western trade, we need to recognize that exchanges never completely ceased between West and East, and that the Byzantine, and above all Muslim, East provided a small quantity of gold in payment for the raw materials which the Christianized and barbarized West continued to supply (timber, iron and slaves). Only long-distance trade with the East maintained a limited circulation of gold in the West, in the form of Byzantine and Muslim coins (respectively, the nomisma, called 'besant' in the West, and the gold dinar and silver dirham). These coins brought some limited wealth to the western rulers (emperors until the end of the Empire in the West, 'barbarian' chiefs become Christian kings, great landowners).

The decline of towns and of long-distance trade fragmented a West where power was largely in the hands of the owners of large estates (*villae*) and the Church. However, the wealth of these new men of power was essentially based on land and on men who had been enserfed or peasants whose independence had been eroded. The rent of these peasants consisted primarily of labour services and renders of agricultural produce, but it also included a small element of cash, which the peasants procured through the intermediary of local markets that were relatively undeveloped. The Church, and in particular the monasteries, hoarded the larger part of the monetary income they obtained from tithes, paid partly in cash, and from the exploitation of their estates. The coins, with the precious metal they contained, and the gold and silver ingots, were turned into plate which was locked away in the treasuries of churches and monasteries to act as a monetary reserve. When the need arose, these objects were melted down to be made into coin. This practice, which spread beyond the Church to the great landowners, and even to kings, highlights the relatively small scale of the cash needs of medieval people. We may also note that it shows, as Marc Bloch shrewdly observed, that the Early Medieval West attached little value to the work of silver- and goldsmiths, or to the beauty of the objects they made. Shortage of cash was thus one of the characteristic weaknesses of the Early Middle Ages in the economic sphere, as a means both to wealth and to power. Bloch also, in his remarkable *Esquisse d'une histoire monétaire de l'Europe*, published in 1954, ten years after his death, emphasized that monetary phenomena dominated economic life, of which they were both a symptom and an effect.

The manufacture and the use of money during this period were increasingly fragmented. We do not yet have a detailed study of all the many sites and regions where mints operated, assuming such a thing is possible.

The people of the Early Middle Ages, who increasingly less often used money, that is, coins, at first retained, and then imitated, the monetary practices of the Romans. Coins were struck with the effigy of the emperor, and the gold shilling, or solidus, continued to be the principal money of exchange. However, to adapt to the fall in production, consumption and trade, the principal gold coin in circulation soon became the triens, that is, a third of a gold shilling. There are several reasons for the continued use, in however diminished a form, of the ancient Roman money. Before their entry into the Roman world and the formation of Christian states, the barbarians had not minted coins, with the exception of the Gauls. Money was for a while one of the few unifying factors because it circulated in all the territories that had once been part of the Roman Empire.

Finally, the weakening of the economy meant that there was little incentive to mint new coins. From the fifth century, at different dates according to the peoples and the new states in question, the barbarian leaders who had gradually taken over the powers of the Roman emperors ended the state monopoly that had once belonged to the emperor. In the case of the Visigoths, it was Leovigild (573–86) who first dared to issue triens with his titulature and effigy on the front; they went on being minted until the Arab conquest at the beginning of the eighth century. In Italy, Theoderic and his Ostrogothic successors had maintained the Roman tradition, and the Lombards, freeing themselves from the Constantinian model, struck coins bearing the name of their king only from the time of Rothari (636–52) and then of Liutprand (712–44), in the form of a shilling of reduced weight. In Great Britain, where coins ceased to be minted around the middle of the fifth century, it was only at the end of the sixth century and beginning of the seventh that the Anglo-Saxons issued, in Kent, gold coins that were copies of Roman coins. Around the middle of the seventh century, gold coins were replaced by silver coins, the sceattas. From the end of the seventh century the kings of the various small British kingdoms tried to reinstate on their own behalf the royal monopoly, in which they succeeded, more or less rapidly and with more or less difficulty, in Northumbria, Mercia and Wessex. We should also, given that the coins of this name were destined to a long and brilliant future, note the appearance in Mercia, in the reign of Offa (757–96), of a new type of coin, the penny.

In Gaul, the sons of Clovis first put their name on the coins of copper that were still issued in their states. Then one of them, Thierry I, king of Austrasia from 511–34, had silver coins struck in his name. However, the true royal monopoly had applied to the minting of gold coins. The first Frankish king bold enough to do this, as Marc Bloch pointed out, was Thierry's son, Theudebert I (534–48). Nevertheless, in Gaul, too, the royal monopoly soon disappeared. By the end of the sixth and beginning of the seventh centuries, the coins no longer bore the name of the king but that of a moneyer, a maker of authorized coins, and the number of moneyers greatly increased. They included palace officials, urban goldsmiths, churches and bishops and great landowners. There were even itinerant moneyers, and it has been estimated that, in Gaul, more than 1,400 moneyers were minting the triens. Three types of metal were used for coin, as in the Roman Empire: bronze or copper, silver and gold. Little is known about the cartography or chronology of the minting of coins in these various metals and, as Marc Bloch observed, it is difficult to understand the reasons for it. In the new states, except in England, where copper and bronze had been common, gold was at first widely used before declining significantly. In fact, gold or, to be more precise, the gold shilling, served largely as a money of account, except among the Salian Franks. Lastly, according to Marc Bloch, a silver coin actually minted under the Roman Empire came to be widely used as a money of account in the so-called 'barbarian' Early Middle Ages; it, too, was destined to a great future: the denier.

2

From Charlemagne to Feudalism

The multiplicity of currencies and fluctuations in the relative value of gold and silver greatly complicated the use of specie in the Early Middle Ages. Charlemagne ended this confusion and created a much more orderly monetary environment within his empire. In fact, reform had already begun in 755 under his father, Pippin. According to Marc Bloch, the three great principles inspiring this reform were the resumption of the minting of coins by the public authorities, the creation of a new system of equivalence between the denier, now real, and the sou (shilling), and the cessation of the striking of gold coins. A period of gold and silver bimetallism was replaced by a period of silver monometallism.

The literature of the Early Middle Ages rarely speaks of the 'rich', a word which meant men of power rather than men of wealth. One of the most famous and most utilized texts in the Middle Ages was the *Etymologies* of Isidore of Seville (c.570–636). In this famous work, Isidore puts love of money first in his list of capital sins. He also dooms the rich to Hell and recalls the Parable of the Rich Man and Lazarus, but he does not condemn riches and the rich outright. Given that wealth was created by God, the rich, if they devoted their riches to the public good and to almsgiving, were justified. In Isidore of Seville too, however, *dives* means a man with power more than a man with a lot of money. We are not yet, in the Early Middle Ages, in the age of money.

Another proof of the dissociation between power and money was the existence in late eighth-century Catalonia of a man who was rich and poor at the same time. He was 'poor' because he was not free; he was a dependent of the king, who, on account of his valour in fighting the Muslims, gave him some newly cleared lands. He was thus made a rich man, although still 'poor'.[1]

A 'natural economy' has sometimes been opposed to a 'money economy' in order to characterize the situation before the diffusion of real money, which became widespread from the eleventh century. Neither of these expressions corresponds to reality. It was only in a very distant past, it seems, that it was possible to lead a self-sufficient life or engage in exchanges involving only produce, men or services. Money circulated in the Early Middle Ages, even among the peasantry, at least in small quantities. Historians have been greatly struck by the appearance in the *Book of Miracles* of St Philibert of a peasant who, at the fair of St Philibert-de-Grand-Lieu, in c.840, went to a tavern to drink half a denier's worth of wine. There are a number of indications of a slow increase in the use of money between the Carolingian and the feudal periods. First, there was the discovery or more active exploitation of the mines producing the metal used for the manufacture of coins. After Charlemagne, this was silver, mostly extracted from argentiferous metals such as lead. The intensive exploitation of the greatest silver mines of the Carolingian period, those of Melle, in Poitou, provided an increased amount of precious metal. The end of the Norman invasions in the ninth century also made it possible to expand the minting of money, as the invaders had primarily pillaged the treasuries of churches, whose contents in gold and silver plate, when melted down, had been one of the main sources of coins, as we have seen. The minting of coins from these raw metals was still a fairly crude process, but effective. The melting process practised in Antiquity had been abandoned and another technique developed: after the preparation of the blanks, that is, the untrimmed body, the coin itself was made by a series of operations comprising the striking, strictly speaking.[2] Towards the end of the Carolingian period, the unit of weight of the coins used in the West, previously based on the Western Roman ounce, was altered and given a new name, though one that concealed many national and regional diversities, that is, the mark. In the territory of medieval France, for example, four types of mark were struck, the most widely utilized being that of Troyes, which weighed 244.75 grams. This mark, used in all the French royal mints, was also sometimes called the mark of the king or mark of Paris.

The emergence of the feudal system, and its evolution towards what Marc Bloch called the second feudal age, not only prepared the ground for the spread of money in the Christian West but also led to the fragmentation of minting and its profits, due to the political and social decadence of the Carolingian Empire. The reforms of Charlemagne had brought about the disappearance of the individual moneyers of the Early Middle Ages, but the imperial monopoly of coinage was short-lived. By the ninth century it had been usurped by the counts, and the 'comital' Middle Ages paved the way for the dispersion of minting that went with feudal fragmentation.

Before the beginning of the tenth century, coins had been issued in Christian Europe only in the lands to the west of the Rhine and in Italy. The emperor Otto I (936–73) created several new mints in the eastern part of his enlarged empire. A Danish mint was established at Hedeby. Coins were struck in Bohemia by 960–5, and in Kievan Rus' by the end of the tenth century. Also by the end of this century, the production of official coins was beginning in the Scandinavian countries (Denmark, Norway and Sweden) while Hungarian coins appeared in the first years of the eleventh century. In the Slav world, coins began to be minted, though on a small scale, in Poland under Mieszko I and Boleslaw Chrobry 'the Brave' (992–1025), most of them imitations of Saxon, Bavarian, Bohemian and Anglo-Saxon coins. Around 1020, coins ceased to be struck in Sweden, Norway, Kievan Rus' and Poland. The earlier issues, in limited quantities, had thus been primarily motivated by political aims and a desire for prestige. The cessation of minting seems to be linked to two factors: the absence of a local supply of precious metals and the weakness of commercial exchanges. In contrast, the minting of coins continued to increase in Saxony, Bavaria, Bohemia and Hungary.[3]

For the coastal regions of the Channel and the North Sea, texts from the early eleventh century attest to the growth of long-distance trade and to the reactions of the Church to their new wealth; I refer to the work of two monks, Aelfric, master of novices at the abbey of Cernel (Cerne Abbas) in Dorset and author c.1003 of a dialogue, the *Colloquy*, and Alpert of Metz, a monk from the Utrecht region, author, between 1021 and 1024, of the *De diversitate temporum*, in which he describes the merchants of Tiel. Alpert is fiercely critical of these merchants, accusing them of numerous vices, and in particular of retaining the securities which some borrowers had been able to provide. Aelfric, by contrast, offers one of the first justifications of the activities of the merchant; he describes himself as 'useful to the king and to ealdormen and to the wealthy and to all people'. He sells his cargo in foreign countries, he says, from which he returns with precious goods that are not to be found in Christendom, risking his life at sea. He mentions clothes of purple and silk, precious stones and gold, spices, oil, ivory, sulphur and glass, and, when asked if he sells his merchandise at the same price that he bought it, he replies: 'I do not wish to. What benefit to me would my labours be then? I want to sell them for a higher price than I bought them, so I get a certain profit and am able to feed myself, my wife and my sons.' We see in embryo what would later be one of the justifications for the profit, the interests of those who earned money: remuneration for labour, compensation for risk, the need for those who do not work on the land to feed themselves.[4]

Around 1050, the term *riche* appeared in old French in place of *dives*, but it essentially retained the meaning of 'powerful'. I believe, therefore, that when Hironori Miyamatsu said that the rich man in the modern sense of the word was about to emerge at the end of the eleventh century, he was exaggerating. It was at this period, however, that there appeared a phenomenon which greatly accelerated the use of money, that is, the crusade. Anticipating long journeys in hostile territory, and not knowing what booty they would find in the Holy Land, many crusaders were anxious to procure money that was easily transportable, that is, of high value and low weight, and lay their hands on as many deniers as they could.

3

The Rise of Coin and Money at the Turn of the Twelfth and Thirteenth Centuries

The changes in the perceptions of money and in its use which marked this period, which was in many respects crucial for medieval societies, were linked to a number of fundamental developments. The most important of these were the transition from the itinerant to the settled merchant; the rise of towns – towns being great makers and consumers of money; the return to a gold currency; the growth of profit and the first attempts to justify it – within certain limits and on certain conditions; the slow shift from total condemnation of usury and usurers to a degree of tolerance of profit, of interest and of those they enriched; the spread of money and of its regulation, primarily due to the strengthening of public and above all monarchic authority; the promotion of the image of work; and the growth in the teaching and practice of law. The paradox is that the increase in the number of rich men and the more tolerant attitude to the accumulation and use of money coexisted, or rather developed, together with a eulogizing of poverty, an increase in charity towards the poor and an association of their image with that of Jesus. The beginning of the thirteenth century was the time both of the canonization (in 1204) of St Homobonus, a rich merchant of Cremona (in fact, in spite of his wealth), and of the glorification of poverty by St Francis of Assisi.

The growth of trade

The growth of long-distance trade, which owed little to the crusades, military ventures of no great benefit to Christendom, was primarily visible, beyond small local or regional markets, in the creation and activities of certain great fairs, which we may call international. The best known, and certainly also most important in the twelfth and thirteenth centuries, were the fairs of Champagne, held at Lagny, Bar-sur-Aube, Provins and Troyes. They followed one after the other throughout the year: Lagny in January–February, Bar in March–April, Provins in May–June, the star attraction being the May Fair, Troyes in July–August, with the most important fair that of St Jean, Provins again in September–November, the high point being the fair of St Ayoul, and Troyes again in November–December, when the chief fair was that of St Remi. The counts of Champagne, on whose territory these fairs were held, ensured the legality and honesty of the transactions and guaranteed the commercial and financial operations. Special officials were established, the 'Guards of the Fair'. This was a public office, though often entrusted to burgesses, until 1284, when the kings of France, who had become masters of Champagne, appointed royal officials. The monitoring of financial operations and the checks on the honesty of the exchanges gave these fairs what has been called 'the role of a clearing-house' in embryo. The practice of contracting and settling debts at them and the growing importance of exchange transactions enhanced the role of fairs, and in particular those of Champagne, in the economic and social life of medieval society. They were primarily a source of wealth for the merchant class, but the impetus they gave to the manipulation of money was of great importance.

The rise of the towns

The other cause of the increase in the circulation of money was the rise of the towns. Of course, the use of money was not unknown in the countryside. Increasingly, in the context of what is called the feudal economy, lords no longer collected rent from their peasants in produce or in labour services but in money, which steadily increased as a proportion of these levies.

While it is inappropriate, therefore, even in relation to the countryside, to talk of a 'natural economy', it is even more inappropriate in relation to the towns. The rise of craft industry stimulated the purchase of raw materials and the sale of manufactured goods, while the increasing use of wage earners, as Bronislaw Geremek showed for thirteenth-century Paris, led to an increase in the use of money in the towns. The rise in the living standards of the urban population created a new social divide, this time between rich burgesses and poor citizens. The crusades did little to stimulate trade with the East, but their financing swallowed up a significant proportion of seigneurial wealth and resulted in a decline in the importance of the landlords in relation to the increasingly wealthy burgesses. The great age of cathedral-building, especially Gothic (twelfth to thirteenth centuries), which a tired cliché has attributed to the work of men offering their labour freely to God, was in reality a massive drain on ecclesiastical and urban finances. It held the towns back from further enrichment, as I will show, even if it is impossible to accept the thesis of Robert S. Lopez, who, in a famous article, claimed that 'this killed that' – 'this' being the cathedrals and 'that' the expansion of the monetary economy. First, we need to add to the construction of the cathedrals that of many churches and castles built of stone, when town houses had almost always been of wood; far from constituting a drag on the monetary economy, as Lopez believed, this was a great stimulus to it. The activities of the urban markets greatly increased in scale and regularity, making it necessary for these commercial centres making use of money to build market halls which often still impress us today. In the Paris of Philip Augustus (1180–1223), major enterprises, such as the construction of the city walls and market halls, testify to this expansion of money.

The acquisition of franchises by the towns freed them from the burden of seigneurial dues, which had held back their economic development and the diffusion of money. The latter was the cement of the associations which were established both within the towns, that is, the guilds, and between prosperous trading towns, that is, the hanses. By this means, certain regions of Christendom experienced an urban and commercial growth which gave them more wealth, more power and a more dazzling image as compared with those where growth was less strong and less money circulated.

Two main regions stand out in this way. The first was the north-east of Europe, from Flanders to the Baltic countries. The towns of this region initially grew rich from the sale of cloth, but their craft production – in the case of textiles, almost industrial production – expanded and diversified. They formed a vast network which was also a major channel for the circulation of money. The richest of these towns were Arras, Ypres, Ghent, Bruges (the most powerful), Hamburg and Lübeck, founded in 1158, with also Riga, founded in 1201, and Stockholm, founded in 1251. To these we should add London, which, by attaching itself to the Hanseatic network, became a major economic centre. The other dominant region was northern Italy and the Mediterranean zone in general. Its great centres were Milan, Venice, Genoa, Pisa and Florence with, in the second rank, Cremona, Piacenza, Pavia, Asti, Siena and Lucca. Genoa was, among other things, the hub of a great slave-market, the latter supplied by the Catalans or Majorcans, as dictated by the Spanish Reconquista, and by the regions bordering the North Sea. It was from Caffa, on the Black Sea, that a Genoese ship embarked for Europe in 1347 carrying the virus of the Black Death. By the thirteenth century, Venice was home to a true glass industry, largely concentrated in the Isle of Murano.

These two areas were joined by newly emerging towns on the Atlantic coast, in particular La Rochelle, seized by the king of France in 1224, and Bordeaux; the latter, after the English established themselves in south-west France, saw an expansion in the production and trade in wine, a new source of wealth. It was not only the wines of Bordeaux that were valued in England, where those of Poitou, exported through La Rochelle, were also highly esteemed and widely drunk. Thirty ships carrying wine from Poitou were shipwrecked off the Channel port of Saint-Valéry-sur-Somme in 1177.

In general, compared with the countryside, where there was little further progress after the twelfth century,[1] the towns were exhibiting dynamism on every front: dynamism of labour, thanks to technological progress, which exploited the energy of urban mills for metallurgy, tanning and even the manufacture of beer; social dynamism too, as, with the possible exception of Italy, where the lords often continued to live in them, the merchants took over the towns, thanks to their businesses and their workers.

Once in a controlling position, they were able to impose their economic and social dynamism thanks to the promotion of the concept of work, which was no longer despised as a consequence of original sin, even if manual labour retained its pejorative connotations. The rise of towns was also one of the basic causes of the increase in the use of coin, and also of currencies, in the twelfth and thirteenth centuries; we should not forget that there was no money market and that the use of a particular currency was not determined by any feeling of identity.

The need for money

The increase in the use of money may have been principally a consequence of urban growth, but it extended well beyond the towns. This was the case with textiles and draperies, which entailed large numbers of purchases, sales and exchanges, even with the world beyond Christendom. This was almost the only sector to reach a quasi-industrial stage and it led to an increase in the circulation of money among the clothiers, who flourished principally in Flanders and Hainault. Nevertheless, though it remained for the most part individual, while benefiting from the considerable technological progress in the weaving trades, some cloth manufacture developed in the countryside and, if we can take as reflecting reality the famous passage in a romance of Chrétien de Troyes, *Erec et Enide* (c.1170), describing weary female silk workers in the workshop of a seigneurial castle, cloth manufacture was carried out in castles too. There were similarities in the case of the building trades. The use of wood declined in favour of stone and metal. The demand for the stone of Caen, for example, was so great from the eleventh to the fifteenth centuries that it was quarried and traded on an industrial scale, which necessitated a considerable use of money; the exploitation of quarries was in general a far greater incentive to the growth of a money economy than that of the forests.[2] Medieval archaeology has recently spread to the countryside in France, on the model of Poland, and excavations have been undertaken in Burgundy, notably in the village of Dracy, in Côte-d'Or. The archaeologist in charge, Jean-Marie Pesez, has emphasized that, exceptionally, the peasant houses there were built not of wood but of stone.[3]

We should note that the turn of the twelfth and thirteenth centuries probably marked the apogee, and soon decline, of the role of the monastic orders in the circulation of money. Some monasteries, in particular those attached to Cluny, had been among the principal moneylenders to the indebted laity. However, the demand for money began to increase to the point where these monasteries were relegated to the sidelines.

Faced with this increased demand for money, Christendom was lacking in internal resources in precious metals, in spite of the exploitation of new mines and in spite of the spread in the north and east of Christian Europe of silver coins of high value, and even of Byzantine and Muslim gold coins. This is why the advance of the monetary economy in the twelfth century remained confined within certain limits, though it is impossible for the historian to estimate with any confidence the importance of money at this period. The lack of communication between economists and numismatists, and the ambiguity of the few written sources, from which we are often unable to tell whether what is mentioned is real money or money of reference, mean that this period in the history of money is largely uncharted territory. Things changed in the thirteenth century. The possibility of a more detailed and more wide-ranging discussion increases in line with the fuller documentation and with the advance of the money economy after the great transformation of the Christian West between 1150 and 1250.

4

The Glorious Thirteenth Century of Money

By 'glorious' thirteenth century, I mean a long thirteenth century, too. In this I am following the great English historian Peter Spufford, who, in 1988, published a book that has become a classic, *Money and its Use in Medieval Europe*. With as his model Fernand Braudel, who wrote of a 'long sixteenth century', Spufford devoted the central section of his book to what he called 'the commercial revolution of the thirteenth century', a century he defined as stretching from c.1160 to c.1330. It is this long thirteenth century that I will discuss in this chapter. Coming after the trends first visible in the twelfth century, and before the difficulties and conflicts which would disrupt the use of money in the fourteenth century, it appears as a high point.

Money under debate

The most visible signs of the debate surrounding money were the fierce argument about lending at interest, which the Church called 'usury', and the way in which the Church's attitude to usurers wavered between a strengthening of the traditional hostility and the beginnings of a degree of tolerance. It was in the thirteenth century that money was the subject of the most sustained theoretical debate in ecclesiastical circles. The prominence of money in theology and in preaching was largely due to three factors: the birth and development of religious orders that were located in the towns rather than in the countryside, that is, the mendicant orders, chief among them the Dominicans and the Franciscans; the growth of preaching in the towns, now in the vernacular, not Latin, and so accessible to large numbers of the faithful; and the university teaching which, by addressing problems of concrete concern to believers here on earth, led to the development of the syntheses, the *summa*, in which money figured. The foundation of the universities was linked to the intellectual, economic and social problems caused by the enhanced role of money in medieval Christendom.

Let us look at a series of sermons delivered, mostly in the vernacular, that is, in German, in Augsburg in 1257 or 1263 by one of the greatest scholastic intellectuals of the thirteenth century, Albert the Great. Albert was a Dominican who, after studying in Padua and Cologne, acquired the title of master of theology at the University of Paris between 1245 and 1248. He then taught at the *studium* of Cologne, where his students included Thomas Aquinas, and preached at various places in Germany until his death, in Cologne in 1280. He was the first great Christian interpreter of the works of Aristotle. His weekly sermon, that is, a series of seven sermons delivered daily over the course of one week, took as their theme the commentary of St Augustine on a sentence in the Gospels: 'A city set on a hill cannot be hid' (Matthew, 5.14). These sermons contained what amounted to a theology and a eulogy of the town. Albert emphasized the role of the merchants and of the rich men who supplied the town with everything it needed and who made it possible both for the poor to survive and for the town to be adorned with the monuments that constituted its beauty. In his list of capital sins (the order in which medieval theologians, moralists and preachers arranged this list is one of the best indicators of their attitude to the social and moral order), the first and the worst is lust; avarice, that is, greed, comes only third in the list. The great American medievalist Lester K. Little shrewdly observed, in his fine book *Religious Poverty and the Profit Economy in Medieval Europe* (1978), that what Albert the Great was saying in his preaching was that the image of Paradise on earth was not the monastic cloister but the town marketplace. He had integrated the growing importance of the town and of money into his thinking.

In contradiction to this phenomenon, there was a significant increase in the number of poor in the towns. Michel Mollat, the great historian of the medieval poor, emphasized that, although the countryside had its poor, it was principally in the towns that there was this new proliferation of poor people in the thirteenth century. He quoted as example Florence, though it is not till the fourteenth century that we have the figures to measure this. I will return to what may appear a contradictory link between the increase in the circulation of money and the increase in almsgiving in monetary form. The obvious cause is the unequal distribution of this increased volume of money, economic prosperity usually being accompanied in historic societies by an increase in social inequality.

The new costs of urban investment

For the lords, the disadvantages of this increase in the circulation of money may have outweighed the advantages, but for the towns it caused serious financial problems. The wealth that resulted from the growth of craft production and more importantly of trade was principally individual or familial. Yet the towns were faced with expenses relating to the community and to the persons and organizations (mayors, magistrates, etc.) that represented them after their emancipation, largely achieved in the twelfth century. They needed, as a result, to establish effective mechanisms for raising taxes. Their heaviest expenditure was on the construction and even more repair of the fortifications that surrounded the majority of towns in this age of violence between lords and princes. As we have seen in the case of Ypres and Paris, the growth of trade meant it was necessary to build a market hall, which was not only a matter of commercial convenience as it came almost to rival the cathedral as symbolic image of the town. At Agde, in 1305, the consuls had to cooperate with the bishop in order to construct in the main square a market hall which was to be 'the highest and widest that could possibly be built'.

Further, private investment was not enough on its own to build ovens, cellars, presses or, most importantly, mills in towns, and it was often necessary for the urban community to intervene. This was the case at Agde, in 1218–19, when both the city and the bishop had to invest in the construction of mills along the River

Hérault. Many towns were also obliged to bear the cost of building aqueducts, wells, canals and fountains. At Provins, in 1273, the mayor arranged for water from outside the town to be piped into the houses and streets; in 1283 the town obtained from the king the right to install four new fountains at the inhabitants' expense. It was also in the thirteenth century that the town houses that would later be called *mairies* (mayoral offices) began to be built. Town halls appeared by the end of the twelfth century, for example in Toulouse between 1190 and 1204. The ordinary expenses of a town such as Bruges included the payment of allowances to the members of its council and the fixed annual wages – called pensions – of some of its officials, that is, of its municipal functionaries. Other expenses included the salaries of the sergeants responsible for policing, the cost of the ceremonial outfits of the council members, the liveries of the municipal employees and the receptions offered to distinguished visitors, which turned into backhanders for persons whose favour the town hoped to win. Lastly, according to Raymond de Roover, the cost of messengers was significant. To this should be added the foundation of hospitals and leper-houses, part of the charitable policies of towns. Jacqueline Caille has convincingly shown what she calls 'the communalization and laicization' of the hospitals of Narbonne.

Another example, also studied by Caille, is that of the money spent by the commune on the construction of bridges. Given that towns were usually located on rivers, the building of bridges was from the beginning, from Rome to Paris, one of the responsibilities and chief expenses of urban authorities. In 1144, when the count of Toulouse founded the new town of Montauban, he made the construction of a bridge over the Tarn, at their own cost, an obligation on the immigrants who came to live there. The Middle Ages was marked by a more or less rapid and more or less widespread transition from timber to stone as the material for these bridges. Stone was more expensive, but it should not be assumed that timber could not prove very costly. It was susceptible to fires, as were most town houses, and it was more vulnerable than stone to the destructive effects of great floods. Three bridges were built in Narbonne, both signs and instruments of the spread of money: the first, called the Pont-Neuf, in 1275, replaced an old bridge believed by historians of Narbonne either to be a twelfth-century or an ancient Roman construction; the second followed in 1329 and the third in 1341. The latter had a timber roadway but masonry piles, as the Pont-Neuf had been partly destroyed by a serious flood in 1307.[1] The cost of these bridges was met in part by the lords of Narbonne and various persons of note for whom they were particularly useful, but primarily by two tolls; these were collected by a farmer who had emerged victorious from an auction by candle. The bidding for this toll was particularly high because it primarily attracted the well-off merchants and craftsmen. The king, although remote, was forced to intervene on several occasions, usually to authorize expenditure in connection with the construction or upkeep of the bridges. They were built right at the end of the apogee of the economic and social expansion of the towns during the long thirteenth century.

Generally speaking, the Middle Ages, whose technological equipment and technical knowledge was less advanced than today, were particularly susceptible to catastrophes such as floods, fires and landslides, which necessitated greater recourse to money for repairs. A detailed history of medieval catastrophes remains to be written, despite the pioneering work of Jacques Berlioz, and it is a gap in the history of the Middle Ages. Though the Church and the people were the principal providers of finance for the urban works at Narbonne, as in many other cities, the role of the viscount was crucial in the minting of the coins used in the town and its hinterland. The high quality of the coins he struck was so important to the inhabitants of Narbonne that Amaury I was obliged in 1265 to proclaim by *ordonnance*, in response to the prayers of the consuls of the *cité* and the *bourg*, that 'he would maintain and preserve all his life the new coins that his father had recently minted.'[2]

Building the cathedrals

Even before all these great works of improvement and maintenance, the building projects which absorbed the most money in the thirteenth century were the great Gothic cathedrals. History long propagated the myth of cathedrals that were the product of faith and of a religious fervour so strong that the mighty procured the essential raw materials to build them at no cost, and the labour was performed by a workforce that was similarly free, whether it consisted of men of servile condition lent by their lords without charge or men of free status who offered their labour to God. The more clear-sighted research of historians of the second half of the twentieth century has shown that the building of the great cathedrals cost dear; and that we may also, as I have already suggested, admire these monuments while at the same time seeing their cost as one of the reasons, together with the crusades and monetary fragmentation, why the European economy failed to take off in the Middle Ages. In 1991, the American historian Henry Kraus addressed this question in a fine book, to which he gave the eloquent title *Gold Was the Mortar. The Economics of Cathedral Building.* He examined how several of the great cathedrals were financed, though inevitably very approximately and in a manner difficult to transpose into modern values, given the paucity of the documents and their lack of detail. They included Notre-Dame in Paris. This was primarily paid for by the Church, which allocated the rent income from, or proceeds of the sale of, some of its lands and temporal goods by gifts of money made by its rich bishops and by the *taille*, a head tax, which the chapter repeatedly imposed during the first period of construction, that is, the late twelfth century. The founding bishop Maurice de Sully (d. 1196), for example, left a bequest of 100 livres to buy lead for the roof of the nave; in c.1270, the rich canon Jean de Paris paid for the building of the transept, and the most generous donor of all, whose gifts totalled more than 5,000 livres, was Bishop Simon Matiffas de Buci (d. 1304).

At Amiens, the main building works, between 1220 and 1250, were funded by the burgesses. Bishop Geoffroy d'Eu sold some of his properties, added to which he prohibited all gifts to other churches in the town while the cathedral was being built. At the end of the thirteenth century, the town took out large loans to cover the cost of completing the building, which significantly increased its debt. The commune also forced the Dominicans, who were established outside the town but owned two houses inside it, to sell them these houses to build a market, the revenues of which were assigned to the cathedral. The money donated by the woad merchants, who had grown rich on this trade, earned them, in gratitude, a fine carving in which they were represented.

Toulouse never succeeded in acquiring a cathedral worthy of the great town it had become, as neither the burgesses nor the Church were ready to invest heavily in building it. Other churches had attracted the attention and the funds of the citizens and the clergy. In the twelfth century, these were the superb Benedictine church of St-Sernin and the churches of la Daurade and la Dalbade, the last two largely financed by the many craftsmen and traders active in their quarters, in particular the guild or confraternity of the cutlers. The period when Toulouse was at the centre of a witch-hunt against the Cathars was hardly propitious to the building of a great cathedral. When Bishop Bernard de L'Isle-Jourdain (1270–86) decided to resume and promote the building of a cathedral, it was the churches of the mendicant orders which attracted the heaviest investment, in particular that of the Dominicans, the church of the Jacobins, which the inhabitants of the city regarded as a 'surrogate cathedral'.

In the case of Lyon, where the construction of the cathedral was resumed in 1167, the financing was once again assured by the same two sources, that is, the clergy and the burgesses. In the event, neither of them showed a sustained and serious enthusiasm in the form of an allocation of resources through bequests or gifts. As a result, the building of the cathedral of St-Jean de Lyon dragged on until the end of the sixteenth century. In contrast, the enthusiasm of the citizens of Strasbourg for their cathedral, a new Gothic construction replacing the Romanesque nave destroyed by fire, allowed the work to make rapid progress in the middle of the thirteenth century, and the great facade was completed between 1277 and 1298. At York, where the archbishops played the main role, the construction of the cathedral after 1220 alternated between periods of intense activity and periods of stagnation.

Kraus also studied the construction of the cathedrals of Poitiers and Rouen. At Poitiers, surprisingly, there was a long lull in building works after the takeover of Poitou by the French in 1242, and this continued through the long years of the appanage of Alphonse de Poitiers, brother of St Louis (d. 1271). In Rouen, the construction of the cathedral was encouraged both by the last English kings and by the French kings, Philip Augustus, Louis VIII and St Louis. However, the latter, in his generosity to church building, was torn between his close friendship with the archbishop of Rouen, Eudes Rigaud, and his strong attraction for the mendicant orders. Like many medieval cathedrals, that of Rouen was only completed in the late fifteenth and early sixteenth centuries; it was then that the famous Tour de Beurre (Butter Tower), so called because it was paid for by the Lenten indulgences bought by the greedy burgesses, was built.

Alongside this funding by ecclesiastical revenues and the donations of the burgesses, what made a rational management of the financing of cathedral building possible, generally from the beginning of the thirteenth century, was the emergence of an ad hoc institution, known as the 'fabric committee' (in France *la fabrique*, in Italy *l'opera*). The 'fabric' was responsible for collecting the revenues, which were usually irregular and of variable size, for ensuring the regular financing of the building works and for drawing up a budget which laid down an overall schema and detailed the various items. According to Alain Erlande-Brandenburg, 'it played the role of regulator, indispensable for the implementation and monitoring of an enterprise on this scale... it had to bring order to a reality that was, as I have already emphasized, anarchic in the extreme'.[3] The most detailed study of the *opera* of an Italian cathedral is that of Andrea Giorgio and Stefano Moscadelli for Siena.[4] The *opera di Santa Maria* of Siena had been founded very early, the first known reference dating from 1190. The donations to the *opera* in the thirteenth century took the form of legacies and gifts in cash. However, the necessary financial basis for the activities of the *opera* and the funding of the cathedral construction was the monopoly of the income from the wax offered to the cathedral or bought by it. The product of this monopoly was largely paid over in cash. This privilege was defined in detail by a legal document, the *Constitutio* of 1262. Lastly, by the end of the thirteenth century the *opera* was provided with an endowment intended to fund the work on the cathedral. It consisted of fields and vineyards outside the town, the profits from the mill of the Ponte di Foiano from 1271, some stretches of woodland for its needs in timber, a few marble quarries and, in the fourteenth century, a steadily expanding portfolio of property in the town. The documents make it possible, lastly, to calculate in some detail the proportion of the *opera*'s income devoted to paying the wages of the master craftsmen and the workers.

The recourse to new sources of finance

To meet these new and considerable needs in capital expenditure and running costs, the towns had generally been authorized to raise funds by the king or lord, that is, in effect, to levy taxes. At the beginning of the fourteenth century, for example, according to Charles Petit-Dutaillis, the towns 'owned houses, which they let at quit-rent, they owned marketplaces, vices, drains, sometimes mills; in fact all kinds of sources of revenue...They pocketed fines, seigneurial dues on property transfers, taxes payable on entering the burgess class or joining a gild. They offered for sale municipal offices and sergenteries' (*The French Communes in the Middle Ages*, p. 126). He goes on to say, however, that all these additional sources of income were not enough to meet their permanent expenses: 'Often they did not amount to a fifth of the budget. The other four-fifths came, at Amiens for example, from annual taxes agreed to in principle by the population and varying from place to place.' The town councils therefore resorted to taxes, either wealth taxes, what we would call direct taxation, then usually called *taille*, or indirect taxes, principally levied on economic activity, which were given various titles but had the generic name of 'aids'. In Bruges, at the beginning of the fourteenth century, there were three aids, called *maltôtes*, that on wine, that on beer and that on mead. The *maltôte* on wine was farmed to moneychangers. In its three forms, this tax provided no less than 85 per cent of the total revenue of the town. The difficulty of raising these taxes, which were highly unpopular, often led the towns to borrow money and fall, consequently, into debt. Patrick Boucheron has spoken of the 'dialectic of borrowing and taxation'. We encounter the public debt in the documents as soon as urban accounts become available, usually in the second half of the thirteenth century in Flanders, northern France and the lands of the Empire. In the fourteenth century it spread to communal Italy, Provence, Catalonia and the kingdom of Valencia. The problems of expenditure and of taxation caused the towns to develop their own urban accounting systems, in imitation of the merchants; these generally appeared in the late thirteenth century, in 1267 in Ypres, for example, and in 1281 in Bruges. The accounts were compiled under the supervision of treasurers, usually wealthy men who, if there was a deficit, had to come up with the funds from their own fortunes. Town accounts were drawn up in the vernacular rather than in Latin and they are among the first documents to have used paper, bought at the fairs of Champagne. The communal accounts of Lille were compiled in 1301 and 1303 on paper.

The finances of a medieval town were usually organized on the basis of a charter of liberties. Lewis Mumford observed that, for the towns, such a charter was the precondition for an effective economic organization. The famous Customs of Lorris, for example, had stipulated in 1155 that no inhabitant of the parish should be required to pay a tax either on products destined for his own consumption or on grain he himself had grown; nor did he have to pay toll at Etampes, Orleans, Milly or Melun.

With the growth of centralized states, such as the county of Flanders and the kingdom of France, urban finances were increasingly controlled. Counts and kings endeavoured to draw up budgets in which, when the texts survive, it is difficult to tell what corresponds to real money and what to a simple valuation. One of the most remarkable attempts to control urban finances was the edict which the king of France, Philip the Bold, issued in 1279 at the request of Count Guy de Dampierre. It instructed the *échevins* (magistrates) of all the Flemish towns to submit annual accounts for the management of their finances before the count or his representatives and in the presence of all interested inhabitants, in particular the representatives of the people and of the community of burgesses. Money thus became an increasingly strong presence in the medieval town. The main aim of the burgesses might be to be free and, in particular, to administer themselves, but their other principal concerns were to do with the management of money. They were no strangers to the feudal system, particularly as, through the urban markets, they provided the lords and their dependent peasant tenants with the money they needed, the former for their expenditure on luxury goods and prestige, the latter to pay part of their rent and to acquire the vital necessities they could not procure in the countryside. However, the burgesses, with an eye to their own comfort and prestige, were beginning to experience the desire to grow rich. They also often employed servants or subordinates to whom they were increasingly obliged to pay wages in cash, as Bronislaw Geremek showed for Paris. These cash resources, as Roberto Lopez has demonstrated, came mostly from trade and manufacture. Of course, only the large towns engaged in long-distance trade were in a position to make widespread and increasing use of money in the thirteenth century. The goods of long-distance trade were grain, wine, salt, leathers and skins, high-quality cloths, minerals and metals.

However, even middling towns were affected by the spread of money: like Laon, which has been called a 'wine capital'; or Rouen, which was a great wine-exporting port, thanks to the privilege it had been granted by the kings of England in the second half of the twelfth century, which was continued by the kings of France in the thirteenth; or Limoges, where the moneychangers had taken over a whole street – the rue des Taules (Street of Tables).

The social effects of monetary growth

Another reason for money to circulate in towns was consumption. I quote the old definition of the great German historian Sombart: 'A town is a settlement of people who rely for their maintenance on the products of foreign (or alien) agricultural labour.' Increasingly, these products were acquired by the townspeople in return for payments in money. A more recent historian, David Nicholas, who has studied the role of consumption in the rise of the Flemish towns, has observed that Flanders was unable to support its own towns and that, in order to feed themselves, the large cities had to ensure they had control of the sources of supply of cereals, thus also protecting themselves against price rises in the grain provided by the small regional centres during frequent periods of shortage. This shows that we should not, I repeat, in the case of the Middle Ages, contrast a rural economy that functioned without money and an urban economy that was external to the functioning of a peasant economy regarded as feudal and non-monetary. Price fluctuations, to which I will return, drew the medieval, and especially the urban, economy even further into the system of prices characteristic of a money economy, even if the prices indicated by our sources do not correspond to real money but are only a fiduciary reference. The use of money in towns was not restricted to the upper echelons of the urban population, the burgesses. It has been calculated that many poor townspeople in mid-fourteenth-century Ghent spent almost half their wages on buying grain and between 60 and 80 per cent of their budget on foodstuffs in general. We should also note that medieval people, and especially those who lived in the towns, consumed a surprising quantity of meat. This is a cultural as much as an economic phenomenon, the reasons for which are not entirely clear. It explains the number and the influence in medieval towns of the butchers, who were, at one and the same time, rich, powerful and scorned. In Toulouse, there were 177 butchers for at most 40,000 inhabitants in 1322, that is, one butcher for every 226 inhabitants, whereas in 1953 the town had a population of 285,000 and 480 butchers, that is, one butcher for every 594 inhabitants.

The circulation and the use of money determined much of the structure of urban society. It was primarily in this context that social inequality appeared in towns, as it appeared in the eyes of thirteenth-century people, and that monetary wealth came to be an increasingly important element in the power of those who ruled the towns. The thirteenth century was the century of the patriciate, the group of families who were better than the rest and who possessed much of the power. Increasingly, the patricians were rich men. Their wealth had three main sources. One, which was traditional, was the possession of land outside the town and of houses inside it; the second, for the most important of them, was trade; the third was a consequence of their privileges and fiscal practices. The rich burgesses managed to avoid paying aids, that is, the indirect taxes. It has been estimated that, in Amiens, the 670 wealthiest inhabitants, who accounted for a quarter of the population, paid only one eighth of the aid on wine. Money makes a very visible appearance in the legal treatises that proliferated in the thirteenth century, which was the age of the revival of Roman law, the appearance of canon law and the transformation of customary law. In the fiftieth chapter, 'Of people in towns', in his Customs of the County of Clermont-en-Beauvaisis, completed in 1283, Philippe de Beaumanoir, royal bailiff, wrote:

> Many disagreements arise in the good towns of communes because of their *taille*, for it often happens that the rich men who manage the business of the town underestimate their own and those of their relatives and exempt the other rich men so they will be exempted themselves, and thus all the expenses fall on the community of the poor.

Finance has been called 'the Achilles heel of the urban communities'. The burgesses, the masters of the town, who were often merchants and financiers, learned how to count in the thirteenth century, which was the century of the rise of numbers and calculation; they also learned how to grow rich by profiting from and encouraging the circulation of money.

It remains difficult, nevertheless, to speak of wealth in the strict sense of the term, even less – a point to which I will return – of capitalists. These men remained 'men of power', and this was equally the case with the Italian merchants and bankers studied, most notably, by Armando Sapori and Yves Renouard. I will take as example a famous man who was the subject of a classic book by Georges Espinas, though it has a title that is, in my view, anachronistic, *The Origins of Capitalism*. This was sire Jehan Boinebroke, a merchant draper in Douai at the end of the thirteenth century. Espinas has shown how Boinebroke dominated the little people of the town, and he clearly owed most of his power to his money, which he lent out, ruthlessly demanding disproportionately large sums in repayment from his debtors. But his power was rooted in other factors too. He provided work, employing directly, in his own workshop or in their homes, workers of both sexes 'whom he paid little, badly or not at all'; he practised the truck system, that is, payment in kind, which incidentally reveals that economic and social life was still not entirely monetized. He owned many lodging houses in which his workers, customers and suppliers lived, thus reinforcing their dependence on him. It has been pointed out that in a town like Lübeck, a great Hanse centre founded in the twelfth century, the commercial buildings, barns, shops, vats, ovens and markets, belonged to a small number of great merchants. Boinebroke was ruthless, lastly, in his use of his political eminence and the power that sprang from it. The increased number of wage earners and role of money in the towns was one of the principal causes of the strikes and riots which appeared around 1280. One of the *échevins* in that year was Jehan Boinebroke who, with his colleagues who belonged to the same social category, repressed a weavers' strike accompanied by acts of violence 'with a cruel energy'.

From the end of the twelfth century, we see an increasing awareness of the value of time among the inhabitants of the towns. The first stirrings of the notion that time is money began to appear. Above all, the thirteenth century put increasing emphasis on the economic, even monetary, value of labour, including manual labour. The growth of an urban wage-earning class was certainly a factor in this. The words of the Gospel, 'the labourer is worthy of his hire' (Luke, 10.7), were frequently quoted. However one right that the urban communities almost never obtained was that – seigneurial and regalian – to mint coins. To assure the successful operation of the economy and to protect their property, therefore, the burgesses often demanded from the lords during the thirteenth century a guarantee of the stability of their currency, as we have seen in the case of Narbonne.

Before we leave the towns, where money 'took off' at the height of the long thirteenth century, we should note, in addition to the major social phenomenon of the opposition between rich and poor, a secondary but significant and unexpected aspect, that is, the way that some women managed to master money and even grow rich. This is revealed by a very precious series of documents for Paris from the beginning of the fourteenth century, the record books of the principal urban tax, the *taille*, for certain years. Among the sources of Parisian wealth was the exploitation of gypsum quarries, the stone from which was used for building – and where there would be mushroom beds long after the Middle Ages. Female owners of these quarries, known as *plâtrières*, or plaster works, were among the most highly taxed Parisians in the late thirteenth and early fourteenth centuries. Dame Marie la Plâtrière and her two children, for example, paid a *taille* of four livres and twelve sous, Houdée la Plâtrière paid a more modest four sous and Ysabel la Plâtrière three, like several others. This allowed Jean Gimpel to observe, not without some exaggeration, that women played a decisive role in the success of the 'cathedral crusade'.[5]

5

Trade, Money and Coin in the Commercial Revolution of the Thirteenth Century

It is generally agreed among medievalists that the expansion of internal and external trade in the West during the long thirteenth century justifies our speaking of a commercial 'revolution'; I have already referred to this. I want now to return to the links between money and this revolution because their significance extends well beyond the purely economic.[1] The margrave Otto of Meissen, whose treasury was seized by the Bohemians in 1189, is here an emblematic figure. He was surnamed 'the Rich' and in his case, exceptionally, the word denoted wealth more than power. One contemporary annalist estimated his wealth in 1189 at more than 30,000 silver marks, principally in the form of silver ingots. It has been calculated that if this treasure had been minted into pfennigs, the most widely circulating coin in that part of Germany at that date, some 10 million of them could have been produced. The ways in which Otto used his wealth illustrate the attitudes of most rich men of his day to money. He invested some in buying land, he financed the construction of new town walls at Leipzig, Eisenberg, Oschatz, Weissenfels and Freiberg, site of the principal mine, and he deposited 3,000 silver marks in the monastery of Zella to be distributed to the churches of the neighbourhood for the safety of his soul. These acts are exemplary in the way they demonstrate the three main uses to which money was put in the thirteenth century, and also the mentality of those who acquired and possessed large quantities of it. First, in a society essentially based on land, landed wealth was the ultimate objective; second, in a period when towns were expanding, their security was an increasingly pressing concern; and third, money, which might, as I will go on to show, have dragged the margrave down to Hell, was used instead on pious works which might contribute to his salvation.

The exploitation of the mines

Generally speaking, the more widespread use of coin, as a consequence of the growth of trade, was made possible by an increased production of argentiferous metals, that is, by the exploitation of new silver mines. However, the productivity of the mines of silver-bearing ore in thirteenth-century Europe never reached the levels it would attain in the fourteenth and fifteenth centuries. It benefited from technical advances, usually coming from Germany and sometimes imported directly by German miners. The Carlisle mines were managed by Germans between 1166 and 1178; eighteen German miners are mentioned in Sardinia in 1160. Much of the silver extracted from these deposits was destined for Venice, in consequence of the city's financial strength and the presence of Germans in the *Fondaco dei Tedeschi*, though the Temple in Paris was supplied in part by silver from the mine of Orzals in Rouergue.

Chief among the newly or more intensively exploited mines were those of Goslar, which provided Albert the Great, the celebrated thirteenth-century Dominican theologian and naturalist, with the material for his treatise on minerals, *De mineralibus*.[2] After Goslar came Freiberg, Friesach, in the Tyrol, Jihlava, in Moravia, the Italian mines of Montieri, near Siena, and Volterra and the mines of Iglesias, in Sardinia, which were dominated by Pisa. In 1257, a Pisan ship carrying 20,000 silver marks, that is, about 5 tons in weight, was taken by the Genoese, who used them to extend their Arsenal. The thirteenth century also saw the discovery of new silver mines in England, in Devon. The ownership and the exploitation of mines were frequently disputed. The margraves of Meissen were able to keep firm control over the mines of Freiberg for a long time, as were the bishops of Volterra in the case of those of Montieri. In Tuscany and Sardinia, the latter dominated by the Pisans, the mines passed into the possession of companies, such as the *compagnie di fatto d'argentiera* in

Montieri and the *communitates fovee* at Massa, which hired the miners and paid them wages. The king of England initially tried to manage the mines of Devon directly, but he too had to resign himself to ceding their exploitation to entrepreneurs. Elsewhere, especially in Italy, the miners were often able to keep the upper hand over the companies exploiting the mines in which they worked, just as in agriculture some peasants retained or won their independence by the fact of being allod-holders or landowners. It was in the mines that, for the first time, in what would become an industry, there appeared worker control.

The circulation of money in Europe

Peter Spufford has attempted to produce a synthetic picture of the respective levels in the use of coin in different parts of Europe in the thirteenth century (what is called the balance of payments) and to measure the flow of silver. The evidence he used, which extended to literary sources, coin hoards and lists of coins, included two texts which date from the end of the period but which, in a sense, both encapsulate it and are its products. They are the first trade and currency manuals drawn up by merchants, one a notebook (*Zibaldone*) compiled in 1320 by a Venetian, da Canal, the other, more structured and closer to a true treatise, the *Practica della mercatura* of the Florentine merchant Franceso Pegolotti, written around 1340.

In 1228, the Venetians constructed a building for the use of German merchants on the Grand Canal, the *Fondaco dei Tedeschi.* This encouraged an influx of Germans, who brought with them the coins from the most productive German mines of the period. The da Canal notebook says the Venice mint was from this point largely supplied with '*L'arçento che vien d'Alemagna*'. Silver from Germany was not only exported to Italy, but reached the Rhineland, the southern Low Countries and Champagne too; from here it spread to France, where it was primarily used for the purchase of foodstuffs. It arrived in the Ile de France in the 1190s. Some of this money had been brought by the Hanseatic merchants, either eastward, through the Baltic, or westward, especially to England. A document of 1242 shows that London was receiving silver plate from Flanders and Brabant and foreign coin from a number of German and Flemish towns, in particular Cologne and Brussels.

The French monarchy grew stronger during the thirteenth century, in particular gaining control of the fairs of Champagne through the marriage of the future Philip IV the Fair to Joan of Champagne in 1284. This made France a major exporter of coin, especially to Italy. In 1296, a third of the taxes raised by the papacy in some dioceses of Tuscany were paid in French money. The circulation of specie between Italy and northern Europe was boosted at the end of the thirteenth century by the opening of regular sea routes, organized by Genoa, Venice and Pisa, and silver in the form of ingots or coin was one of the principal goods transported. Depending on the number and the frequency of these ship movements, a town like Bruges experienced a *strettezza*, or scarcity of money, in June and December and, by contrast, a *larghezza*, or abundance of it, in August and September.

The author of the *Practica della mercatura*, Franceso Pegolotti, is a good example of a man serving a bank that was operating in the institutional and geographical context produced by the long thirteenth century of money. He was the foreign representative of the famous Florentine bank of the Bardi. He managed the office in Antwerp from 1315 to 1317, the London office from 1317 to 1321 and then that of Famagusta, in Cyprus. His business was closely bound up with the trade in certain goods, furs, copper from Goslar, wool from England passing through Venice, salt sturgeon sold in Antwerp and blue carbonate of copper sold in Alexandria. Tuscany was largely supplied with silver (metal) from central Europe, from Montieri in Tuscany or from Iglesias in Sardinia, *argento sardesco* going to Pisa in particular. The Tuscans, in monetizing the silver they acquired, increased its value, either by selling it much more dearly than they had bought it or by investing it in manufactured goods such as the silk cloth produced in Lucca. The Milanese also added value to the silver ingots they obtained by financing the manufacture of metal and cotton goods.

Other trade routes developed between northern Italy and Tuscany and the East, that is, Constantinople, Palestine and Egypt. European silver was both a commodity and a source of finance for the establishments comparable to the fonduks set up by the Easterners in Venice, Acre and Alexandria. The principal coins exported to the East in the thirteenth century were English sterlings, French deniers tournois and Venetian grossi. The increase in the quantity of coin was a direct consequence of the growing volume of exports and re-exports of eastern goods to Europe by the Italians. Two eastern imports to the West assumed particular importance: cotton from northern Syria and spices from India and Arabia. The Pisans, Venetians and Genoese established in Alexandria, Damietta, Aleppo and Acre arranged the transport of these goods from the East to the West. Thus western silver financed the trade in eastern products carried over very long distances. Goods from rather closer at hand, such as Russian furs and the alum of Asia Minor, were joined during the long thirteenth century by silk from China, spices from the East Indies, spices and precious stones from India and pearls from the Persian Gulf. We catch a glimpse here of one of the reasons for the increased flow of silver within and through the West in the thirteenth century, that is, the growth of luxury in western society, seigneurial but also and primarily urban, in the upper ranks of the burgesses.

Religion was another stimulus to the use of money at this period. This was first a consequence of the growth of the papal state, which aroused the indignation of many Christians, in particular among the Franciscans and their followers; I will discuss this more fully later. Many texts fiercely critical of the papacy's liking for money circulated, especially in the late twelfth and early thirteenth centuries, including *Le Besan de Dieu* ('God's Besant'), *Le Roman de carité* ('The Romance of Charity') and, most notably, the parodic *Evangile selon le marc d'argent* ('The Gospel according to the Silver Mark'). Once installed in Avignon at the beginning of the fourteenth century, the papacy took advantage of the geographical location of this town, more central than that of Rome, to step up its financial demands on the Church and the Christians of Europe. Under the pontificate of John XXII (1316–34) the revenues of the Holy See rose to an annual average of 228,000 Florentine florins. This figure seems enormous, and many Christians picturing the wealth of the papacy, though ignorant of the details, concluded that it was a worshipper of Mammon rather than of God. Yet its income was smaller than that of the communal government of Florence and less than half that of the kings of France or England at the same period. In spite of the size of these sums, which made it possible, most notably, to build the papal palace in Avignon, it should be noted that a large part of the revenues of the Apostolic Camera left for or returned to Italy, where the papacy was often engaged in difficult wars. In fact, war in the Middle Ages was hugely expensive, as we will see, and swallowed up large amounts of cash. At the end of the thirteenth century, the Franco-English war in Gascony, precursor to the Hundred Years War, necessitated heavy expenditure on the part of the kings of France and England. Between 1294 and 1298, Edward I spent £750,000 on this war, paying his troops, assuring the defence of Gascony against Philip IV and buying the support or neutrality of many French princes. Returning to Avignon, we need to add to the money raised and spent by the Apostolic Camera the revenues and expenditure of the cardinals of the curia, which was on a huge scale.

Another expense linked to religion during the long thirteenth century was the financing of the final crusades. Lastly, there was the increase in pilgrimages, fairly local, like that of Rocamadour in southern France, but most of all that of St James of Compostella, which attracted an increasing number of pilgrims from all over Europe, including Scandinavia and the Slav countries, and drained large sums of money.

For the French, the beginning of the Italian adventures, which St Louis had rejected but which attracted both his brother Charles of Anjou and his great-nephew Charles of Valois, as well as wealthy French princes, represented a new drain on the finances of royal and seigneurial French society, replacing that of the crusades. The Italian horizon, which began to replace the Palestinian, only made further inroads into French wealth. As for England, its involvement in Germany in the thirteenth century caused large sums of money to flow in that direction. Initially this was due to the massive financial support given by King John to his brother-in-law the emperor Otto IV, defeated at Bouvines. Then Henry III, who married his sister Isabella to the emperor Frederick II, not only spent the whole of a very generous dowry but also gave significant financial support to the emperor in his arduous campaigns in Germany and the Two Sicilies. One example of this bleeding of English wealth by the Germans is provided by the archbishop of Cologne: made rich by the English who had sought his political support, in 1214 he sent 500 marks to Rome, most of it in sterlings. At this same period, the use of money in England was widely disrupted by the circulation of false sterlings minted on the Continent.

While the minting of silver was increasing in Europe, that of gold was developing in Africa. Its exports to Europe (mostly to the east) had previously been hoarded rather than turned into money. African gold, called 'gold of the Sudan', was principally mined south of Morocco, in the northern Sahara, in a region whose chief centre was Sidjilmasa, which had been founded in the eighth century when the trans-Saharan route was opened up. This gold was mostly exported in the form of dust, that is, raw gold in very fine grains. A small amount of African gold left Timbuktu in the form of ingots, but most of it was made into gold coins struck in the Muslim mints of North Africa. Some went to the Muslim Spain of the caliphate of Cordova, from which a little reached adjoining Christian Spain, in particular Catalonia. When the last of the Almoravid rulers of Spain, Mohamed ben Saad, ceased to mint gold coins at Murcia, in 1170, the king of Castile, Alfonso VIII, began to mint his own morabetinos, or maravedis, at Toledo; some of these came into the hands of Italian merchants and reached northern Italy. However, as we will see, in the middle of the thirteenth century gold from the Sahara almost completely ceased to arrive in the Christian countries, which had once again begun to mint gold coins, for the first time since Charlemagne.

Minting, mints and types of coin

Thanks to the exploitation of the new silver or argentiferous lead mines referred to above, large and rapidly increasing amounts of monetized silver began to circulate in Europe. In 1130, there were nine mints in the great mining region of Freiberg, in Saxony, at the foot of the Erzgebirge; by 1197, the number had risen to twenty-five, and, by 1250, to forty. A similar increase has been noted for Italy, in particular for Tuscany, home of the mines of Montieri and other Colline Metallifere (metal-bearing hills). In 1135, there had been only a single Tuscan mint, at Lucca, but by the middle of the century mints had appeared in Pisa and Volterra, too. A new mint was opened in Siena around 1180, which was the basis of the town's subsequent prosperity. In the last decade of the thirteenth century, it was the turn of Arezzo, and then Florence. Of all the coins struck in these mints, it was the deniers of Pisa that were most numerous and circulated most widely. There was a similar monetary expansion in northern Italy. In addition to the old mints in Milan, Pavia and Verona, new ones were established between 1138 and 1200 at Genoa, Asti, Piacenza, Cremona, Ancona, Brescia, Bologna, Ferrara and Menton. In Latium, where there had been only four mints in 1130, the number had risen to twenty-six by 1200; there was even a mint in Rome itself.

In France, the principal regions of new mint creation were Artois and, most importantly, Languedoc, the latter promoted by the bishops of Maguelonne in their capacity as counts of Melgueil; the deniers minted here even crossed the Pyrenees. Though relatively few new mints were set up in central France, the quantities of the principal coins in circulation greatly increased, that is, the deniers tournois of the abbot of St Martin of Tours, the Parisian deniers of the kings and the deniers provinois (from Provins) of the counts of Champagne, whose possessions were annexed to the royal demesne at the end of the thirteenth century.

In the Rhineland, it was the pfennigs of Cologne that were dominant, while in Flanders, in the second half of the thirteenth century, the minting of coins was concentrated in Bruges and Ghent. In England, two large mints dominated, those of London and Canterbury, but many smaller mints were opened for the recoinages of 1248–50, 1279–81 and 1300–2. Lastly, we should note the rapid rise of Kutná Hora, in Bohemia.

The growth of these new mints led to a reorganization and an increase in the number of persons employed, who included wardens, masters and auditors as well as technicians and workers. The mints became, in the thirteenth century, the prototype of the new 'factories' which appeared in some towns. This is why the greatest lords and above all sovereigns increasingly tried to manage the production of coins in the mints that were directly under their control, as in France with Philip Augustus. In Venice in the late twelfth and early thirteenth centuries, the doges of the Republic attempted, often with some success, to free themselves from imperial meddling in the striking of coins. We should remember that medieval people had taken from the Latin the two meanings of the term *ratio*. The word meant reason, but also calculation. The improvements in minting and the spread of coin in the thirteenth century reinforced the use of the term in the second sense and also caused rationalization and calculation to progress in unison. Money was a tool of rationalization.[3] In Venice and in Florence, stewardship of the mints was similar to the exercise of a public office. The royal mints in France were in the hands of farmers who negotiated a lease with the monetary authorities which specified the quantities to be struck, the division of the profits between the mintmaster and the king, the technical conditions and the margin of waste acceptable in the manufacturing process. Each operation was subject to numerous checks – weighing, assay – and registers had to be kept by the mintmaster or his clerks and by the wardens acting for the king, most of which, sadly, have not survived.

The sums of money put into circulation increased significantly, at least in the relatively few cases where we have access to documents that make it possible to measure this. In the years 1247–50, the mints of London and Canterbury struck some 70 million new pennies, worth around £300,000. It is likely that in the order of 100 million pennies, worth some £400,000, were in circulation in the mid-thirteenth century. A generation later, in 1279–81, the same two mints struck 120 million new pennies, worth some £500,000. Edward I, as we have seen, was able to raise £750,000 for the war in Gascony.

In France, in the years 1309–12 for which accounts survive, the Paris mint struck coins worth 13,200 livres tournois per month, that of Montreuil-Bonnin 7,000, that of Toulouse 4,700, that of Sommières-Montpellier 4,500, that of Rouen 4,000, that of St Pourçain 3,000, that of Troyes 2,800 and that of Tournai 2,300. Finally, the principal rulers with an actual or theoretical monopoly of the minting of money began in the thirteenth century to lease at least some minting to mintmasters. The mint at Montreuil-Bonnin was leased in this way in 1253 by Alphonse of Poitiers, brother of St Louis, the agreement providing for 8 million deniers to be struck. A lease arranged by another of the king's brothers, Charles of Anjou, specified the minting of 30 million deniers tournois over a five-year period. It was not always the mintmasters who took these leases. Some went to foreign entrepreneurs, increasingly often Lombards, that is, merchants or bankers from northern Italy. In 1305, the right to mint 30 million deniers tournois in the Périgord mint was leased for five years to two Florentine entrepreneurs.

The increase in the minting of coins in many European countries in the thirteenth century did not put a stop to the practice of using ingots of precious metal to make major payments, either locally or internationally. As with coins, the circulation of these ingots greatly increased in the fourteenth century. Once installed in Avignon, the papacy frequently arranged for the sums owed by churches in various parts of Europe to be sent to it in the form of ingots, which were easier to transport than coins. So many silver ingots were delivered to Avignon during the papacy of John XXII (1316–34) that it was calculated, on his death, that he had received over 4,800 silver marks in the form of ingots in this eighteen-year period, that is, more than a metric ton. The crusades of St Louis in the mid-thirteenth century were to a large extent financed by ingots of silver. These ingots also circulated widely in the thirteenth century in Flanders and Artois, in the Rhineland, in Languedoc, in the Rhone valley, and even in Italy, where coins were not in short supply and money circulated in abundance. It was in silver ingots, for example, that Pisa, defeated by Genoa at the famous battle of Meloria in 1288, paid its fine of 20,000 marks. In central, eastern and northern Europe, the circulation of silver in the form of ingots increased because the monarchies and states of these regions had more need for money than the mass of the population, who scarcely used it in daily life. This was the case in Denmark, the Baltic, Poland and Hungary. Towards the end of the thirteenth century, most of the great trading regions of Christendom began to regulate and tax the circulation and monetization of silver ingots, like Venice in 1273 and the Low Countries in 1299. Many silver ingots were identifiable by the civic emblems of guarantee stamped on them. Three main different types of ingot circulated in Europe in the thirteenth century, varying in their degree of fineness. Elsewhere, a model of Asiatic origin prevailed in the Mediterranean and Black Sea area and a third model in Nordic Europe. In Russia, two different types of ingot circulated, one called Kievan, the other of Novgorod.

Another monetary sign of the increased demand for coin on the part of the trade of each country and of Christendom as a whole was the appearance of new silver coins, with a higher silver content, the grossi; these were first minted, hardly surprisingly given its role in international trade, in northern Italy.[4] Though Frederick Barbarossa had in 1162 produced in Milan an imperial denier containing twice as much silver as previous issues, the first true grosso was struck in Venice between 1194 and 1201, and the 40,000 silver marks sent by the crusaders to Venice were turned into these coins. The weight and price of the new coin – fixed at twenty-six piccolo (or 'little ones') – was integrated into a true monetary system in which deniers and grossi were linked to the Byzantine hyperpyron. Genoa started minting grossi at the beginning of the thirteenth century, followed by Marseille in 1218, the cities of Tuscany in the 1230s and, finally, Verona, Trent and the Tyrol. In 1253, grossi worth a soldo, that is, twelve deniers, were struck in Rome. Charles of Anjou followed suit in his states in southern Italy and in Naples; his carlini, or gigliati, competed with the matapans (or grossi) of Venice. St Louis minted the gros tournois in 1266. Grossi were not produced in the Low Countries or the Rhineland until the beginning of the fourteenth century, as silver coins of lesser value were preferred, to suit a less flourishing trade. It was not until 1350 that a groat began to be struck in England. In contrast, in the Mediterranean region, every town had a silver grosso by the end of the thirteenth century, including Montpellier and Barcelona.

The silver grosso was certainly the most useful and the most used new coin. However, the most spectacular event in the monetary sphere in thirteenth-century Christendom was the resumption of the minting of gold, which had persisted only on the margins of Europe and on a small scale, in the service of relations with the Byzantines and the Muslims. This had been the case in Salerno, Amalfi, Sicily, Castile and Portugal. As already noted, these gold coins had for the most part been minted from African gold dust from the Sudan or Sidjilmasa, south of Morocco. They had been struck in North Africa, in Marrakesh, but more especially in Tunis and Alexandria. This helped to attract St Louis to the region on his two crusades, with the intention of destroying the mints in question.

In Europe, the first gold coins were the augustales struck in Sicily, from 1231, by the emperor Frederick II. However, these coins were linked to the marginal gold currencies in contact with

African gold and the Byzantine and Muslim countries. The first true new gold coins in Europe appeared in 1252 in Genoa and Florence. These were the genovino, or genoin, and the florin (fiorino d'oro), adorned, respectively, with the image of St John Baptist and the fleur-de-lis. From 1284, Venice struck its ducats with the image of Christ and that of St Mark blessing the doge; these coins circulated unrivalled in the Mediterranean. The gold coins of Henry III of England and of Louis IX of France around 1260 were failures. The symbolic images represented on these coins of high value entered into the medieval imagination.

We should not forget a third level of monetary circulation, which also greatly increased in the thirteenth century, that of the low-value billon, coins that suited the needs of everyday life, in particular in the towns. They were often called 'black money'. In Venice, the doge Enrico Dandolo had half-deniers or oboles struck at the beginning of the thirteenth century. At the end of the long thirteenth century, the coin most frequently struck in Florence was the quattrino, or 4-denarii piece, equivalent to the price of a standard loaf of bread. This small change also became the norm for almsgiving, which expanded in the thirteenth century due both to the natural development of society and the influence of the preaching of the mendicant orders. On the French royal demesne, the denier parisis became the *denier de l'aumosnerie*, or 'almoner's penny'; St Louis was a greater hander-out of small change to the poor.

As the minting of gold was added to that of silver, bimetallism was restored, or rather, to use the useful term of Alain Guerreau, trimetallism; historians have paid too little attention to the growing importance of coins of low value, usually of copper, like billon, which testify both to the spread of the use of money at almost every level of the population and to the growth in the number of petty transactions. The countryside was not insulated from this trend, contrary to a received idea, and feudalism, in its second phase as described by Marc Bloch, was permeated by money. By 1170, for example, in Picardy, rents and the new dues were usually fixed in deniers or in monetary value.[5] Between 1220 and 1250, in many parts of Europe, most of the obligations on rural holdings could be commuted and paid in cash. Rich peasants did this and, even though there was, as we will see, no true land market, purchases of land contributed to the formation of a category of well-off peasants – the use of money is always associated with social transformations. When we add the payment in coins of low value for an increasing number of products, we see that money truly assumed its role as store of value in the thirteenth century. There was also a revival and growth of thesauration, the extreme example of which must surely be the Brussels Hoard, consisting of over 140,000 coins buried around 1264. The proportion of pennies, that is, coins in common use, increased in these hoards. Though monetary circulation remained fragmented, it was organized within a regional framework, the various coins circulating within a certain area having more or less fixed values in relation to each other. Monetary historians have seen the long thirteenth century in Germany as 'the period of the regional pfennig'.

This regionalization of the circulation of money led to the appearance of a new category of professional moneychangers, who became so numerous that they occupied an increasingly prominent position in society. Their wealth and prestige was so great at Chartres, for example, that they were able to pay for two of the famous windows in the Gothic cathedral. One of the oldest examples of trade statutes for moneychangers appeared at Saint-Gilles in 1178; it records 133 names. The courtly romance of Galeran de Bretagne has left us a vivid picture of the moneychangers of Metz around 1220:

> So these are the changers in a row
> With their money in front of them:
> One changes, one counts, one says no,
> One says, 'It's true', another 'It's a lie'.
> Never in his wildest dreams did a dozy drunkard
> See what he who is wide awake can see here.
> He is hardly selling for peanuts,
> This one who offers precious stones
> And images of gold and silver.
> Others have before them a great treasury
> Of their rich plate.

Yet it was not until 1299 that the moneychangers of Florence received their statutes and there were only four posts of public moneychanger in Bruges; and in Paris, while the trade was closely supervised, it lacked a proper organization, even though the changers were part of the urban elite and in this capacity took part in processions and other princely entries. As we will see throughout this book, the use of money and the status of the specialists in money oscillated in the Middle Ages between, on the one hand, suspicion and, on the other, social advancement. If suspicion was deepened for some reason, it could turn to contempt and even hatred. This happened in the case of the Jews. Long the chief moneylenders to the indebted poor, they were supplanted in this role by Christians and confined to the role of small-time lenders, but continued to incarnate the evil side of money; and the biblical and gospel contempt for money made them, to this day, its accursed ones.

The rise in taxes and its causes

This relative expansion of coin may have represented progress, but it also had the effect of an increasing inflation, which presented major problems for lords and landowners whose need for cash continued to grow. Kings and princes took advantage of the strengthening of their power over their own estates and then kingdoms, and of administrative systems at their sole disposal (such as the provosts, bailiffs and seneschals of France), to step up the pressure on their subjects so as to obtain revenues in money. As they were still unable to impose regular taxes, they levied a range of dues and commuted into cash the rents they were owed in kind. This was one of the foundations of the growth of their power. The policy was systematically imposed in the county of Flanders by 1187 and in the kingdom of France under Philip Augustus. Those towns which had acquired their administrative and financial independence, particularly in the Low Countries and Italy, pursued a similar policy. The cities in possession of a territory exploited it to their own advantage. In 1280, the town of Pistoia in Tuscany taxed its peasants six times more heavily than its own citizens. The last quarter of the twelfth century saw the appearance of an institution which was slow to develop but which clearly reveals that money and feudalism were not incompatible. Some lords granted to certain vassals fiefs that consisted not of land or services but of an annuity, which were known as fief-rentes or 'money fiefs'. A remote antecedent of this practice has been discovered: in 996, the church of Utrecht enfeoffed a knight not with land but with 12 livres of deniers, payable annually. The fief-rente made rapid progress in the Low Countries, especially from the end of the twelfth century.

The underlying causes of this increased circulation of money were economic and commercial activity, especially the latter. However, the heaviest monetary expenditure in the Middle Ages was probably on that quasi-permanent activity, war. It has been shown that war was more sparing of men than is generally believed. This was because the enhanced importance of money made it more profitable to take the enemy prisoner and ransom him than kill him – we need only think of Richard the Lionheart's ransom on his return from the Holy Land, or that of St Louis, a prisoner of the Muslims in Egypt, both of which involved huge sums. Also, the preparation and equipping of armies was hugely expensive. King John of England was not himself present at the battle of Bouvines (1214), but he provided 40,000 silver marks to pay for the armies of his allies. I have pointed out elsewhere that, as Georges Duby so brilliantly showed, tournaments, those great chivalric festivals, which survived all the attempts of the Church to prohibit them, were in effect great markets, comparable to the major sporting events of today, in which money played a crucial role. Another cause of high spending was the increasingly luxurious lifestyle adopted, most notably, by royal and princely courts and the urban bourgeoisie. At the end of the thirteenth century, the increase in luxury expenditure, for example on spices and refined foods, expensive clothes, often of silk or fur, worn especially by women, and payments to troubadours, trouvères and minstrels, led some kings and princes and some communes to publish sumptuary laws aimed at curbing these excesses. In 1294, Philip the Fair issued an *ordonnance* 'touching superfluities in dress' which was primarily aimed at the burgesses: neither men nor women were any longer permitted to wear furs, objects of gold, precious stones, headdresses of gold or silver or robes worth, in the case of men, more than 2,000 livres tournois or, in that of women, 1,600 livres tournois. In fourteenth-century Tuscany, urban statutes strictly prohibited lavish spending on weddings, including on clothes, presents, banquets and nuptial processions.[6] In 1368, Charles V forbade the notorious shoes *à la poulaine*, with their exaggeratedly long pointed toes, though seemingly with little success.

It is significant that in the cathedral of Amiens, built in the thirteenth century, there is, as we have seen, a small statue representing two woad merchants, that is, traders in a dyestuff that was much more widely cultivated thanks to the growing demand for clothes of blue. So, here we have fashion, luxury and the money to be made from it on view in a sacred building!

6

Money and the Nascent States

One of the spheres in which the rise of money is most visible in the apogee of the long thirteenth century is the construction of what historiography calls the state. The state had not wholly emerged from feudalism in the thirteenth and fourteenth centuries – this, as is well known, would finally happen only with the French Revolution. However, the power of the monarchy, the emergence of representative institutions and the development of the law and of government mark a decisive stage in state formation. In particular, the state played a major role in a sphere in which money assumed special importance in the thirteenth century: taxation. In addition to seigneurial rent, princes and kings generally derived their income from three main sources: from their own demesne, from the profits of the generally accepted prerogative of minting and from the levying of specific taxes.

Financial administration

The most precocious and the most dictatorial of these states, and the one most plentifully supplied with money, was the Church, that is, the Holy See. The Holy See received part of its income from the lands and towns that were under direct pontifical rule, what was called the Patrimony of St Peter. It also collected a tithe from the whole of Christendom. In fact, the tithe did not come to the Holy See itself, as it was used, all over Christendom, to provide for the subsistence of the clergy, ensure the upkeep of churches and support the poor. With the general rise in monetary expenditure, the tithe was paid with increasing reluctance. A reminder of its obligatory nature was issued, accordingly, in Canon 32 of the Fourth Lateran Council (1215), which also fixed a minimum sum to be paid to the Church. In the thirteenth century, the newly reorganized Apostolic Camera provided the pope and the pontifical curia with the income from the various sources on which they depended, that is, feudal rents in kind, the revenues from the collation of benefices and the income from benefices without an incumbent, during the period of vacancy.

At the end of the eleventh century, the pontifical curia had for a while entrusted the administration of its finances to the very powerful order of Cluny. Then, in the twelfth century, the papacy put the reception and transfer of rents, revenues and donations under the control of the financial administration of the Roman curia. Pope Innocent III (1198–1216) put at the head of this Camera a cardinal who lived nearby, in the Lateran. It was the *camerarius* (Cardinal Camerlengo) who was responsible for the administration of the landed patrimony of the States of the Church and for receiving the revenues of the Roman Church and managing the papal palaces. The Council of Vienne (1311) decided that the College of Cardinals should appoint a new Camerlengo on the death of each pope for as long as the Apostolic See was vacant. From the thirteenth century, the papacy turned, for the administration of its finances, to bankers who were not part of the Church but bore the title of moneychanger of the Camera (*campsor camerae*), and then, from the papacy of Urban IV (1261–4), to merchants of the Chamber or merchants of the lord pope (*mercatores camerae* or *mercatores domini papae*). Gregory X (1271–6) brought bankers from his hometown of Piacenza to the curia, the Scotti. At the end of the thirteenth century, the most important companies of papal bankers were the Mozzi, the Spini and the Chiarenti. They were responsible for making all payments on behalf of the Camera. Here, too, growing needs in cash led the papacy to seek new revenues, for example payment for indulgences. These had been granted by the popes since the existence, from the late twelfth century, of Purgatory, which was recognized as dogma at the Second Council of Lyon in 1274. As is well known, the selling of indulgences was one of the reasons given by Luther for leaving the Church in the sixteenth century. The high point in the organization of the finances and tax system of the pontifical state came in the fourteenth century, under the Avignon popes, as we will see. These advances in the management of money, which assumed an increasingly important role in the pontifical state, led St Louis, in 1247, to send the pope a virulent letter accusing the papacy of having become a temple to money, a sign both of the latter's advance and of the resistance it encountered.

In the thirteenth century, a specialist administration of the royal finances gradually developed in the principal Christian monarchies. As was often the case, the most precocious in this regard was the English monarchy, which transported to England and then refined pioneering institutions which had originated in the duchy of Normandy. By the twelfth century, Henry II (1154–89), rightly described as the first 'monetary king of Europe', had established an administration which, as it used a large chequered table resembling a chessboard (the game of chess – or *esches* – was newly imported into the West from the East in the twelfth century), was called the Exchequer; it was described around 1179 by Richard FitzNeal in his *Dialogue of the Exchequer*. It consisted of two departments; one received and paid out sums of money, the other was a sort of court of accounts where the sums were monitored. The head of the Exchequer was the Treasurer, an ecclesiastic up to the end of the fourteenth century. Below him were four barons of the Exchequer and two deputy chamberlains. The accounts were recorded on rolls, the Pipe Rolls, which survive in a continuous sequence from the reign of Henry II. This amounted, according to Jean-Philippe Genet, to 'the most precocious and one of the most sophisticated administrations created by the monarchies of the West'.

In his famous treatise on government, the *Policraticus*, the first great medieval work of political philosophy, John of Salisbury, who was one of Henry II's counsellors, discusses the question of royal taxation. For him, this was not a matter of economics, a concept which did not exist in his day, but of justice. It was incumbent on the king to assure and control the circulation of money, not in his own interests but in those of all the subjects of his kingdom. It was not the wealth of the government that mattered, but good government, in the interests of all subjects. Royal taxation was a question of political ethics, not of economics.[1]

The monetary unification of Brittany around the denier with the *croix ancrée* (anchor cross) and the denier of Guingamp (guingampois) was probably, by the end of the twelfth century, another precocious case of princely monetary policy. Catalonia and Aragon in 1174 and the county of Toulouse in 1178 are analogous cases.

France

The king of France was slower to organize the administration of his finances. This was embarked on in systematic fashion under Philip Augustus at the beginning of the thirteenth century; rapid progress was then made under St Louis (1226–1270). It was only at the end of the thirteenth century that a branch of the royal court was split off to form the Chambre des comptes (Court of Accounts). This was regularized under Philip IV the Fair (1285–1314) and formally confirmed by Philip V the Tall by the *ordonnance* of Vivier-en-Brie (1320). It had two principal functions: to audit the accounts and to control all aspects of the administration of the demesne.

The royal demesne was the main source of the king's income. In the expression of the age, he 'lived off his own'. Other resources became important in the thirteenth century: the rights derived from the exercise of royal sovereignty (royal letters, letters of ennoblement), royal justice and the minting of royal coins. These revenues were not enough to meet the growing needs of the expanding monarchic state, so Philip the Fair tried to introduce permanent royal taxes and create extraordinary taxes. An attempt to institute an indirect tax on exports, markets and merchandise – a tax christened the *maltôte*, or 'wrongly levied' – met with a very hostile reception, especially because it involved fiscal controls in the home; it was a failure. The government then tried direct taxes on acquired wealth, income, the family group and the 'hearth' or homestead (*fouage*). All these attempts came to nothing; the medieval state failed to establish a solid or adequate financial base for its transformation into a modern state. Money remained the Achilles heel of the monarchic construction in France, but also more generally in Christendom as a whole.

France in the thirteenth century, and the reign of St Louis (1226–70) in particular, offers a good example of the involvement of a government in the monetary sphere, that is, in the financing of its activities, in its conduct as a moneyer of a special type – because claiming a superior authority, even royal monopoly, to mint coins – and in its organization of monarchic finances. St Louis took his most decisive action in this sphere at the end of his reign, in the late 1260s, when the new role assumed by money and the problems this caused had become apparent all over Christendom.

The king decided to act through *ordonnances*, the choice of this major act in itself revealing the importance of the currency to the government of a thirteenth-century monarchy. He used a series of *ordonnances* to effect a major reorganization of both the minting and circulation of coin in France and of the king's role in these matters. For Marc Bloch, the most crucial of these *ordonnances* was that of 1262, which laid down two principles: the king's currency was valid throughout the kingdom and that of those lords with the right to mint was valid only in their own lands. Two further *ordonnances*, in 1265, clarified that of 1262. Another, of July 1266, decreed that the minting of the denier parisis should be resumed and that a gros tournois should be launched. Finally, a lost *ordonnance* of between 1266 and 1270 created the gold écu, which I will discuss below.

However Louis IX had taken an interest in the currency in his kingdom well before 1266. He had issued only the denier tournois, but taken steps to ensure that his coins enjoyed a privileged circulation in the kingdom and decreed a series of measures concerning the circulation of money. These were, as listed by Etienne Fournial:[2]

1 In 1263, the tournois and the parisis (the latter not struck since the death of Philip Augustus in 1223) must circulate and be accepted in payment of debts owed to the king.
2 In 1265, the relative value between the two coins was fixed at two tournois for one parisis.
3 At a time when it was common for coins to be imitated, the king prohibited counterfeit deniers that copied his own, that is, the poitevins, provençaux and toulousains, one sign among many that the French monarchy, firmly based in the north, was imposing itself on southern France in this sphere, too.

4 'Because the people believe that there are not enough tournois and parisis coins', the circulation of the nantois *à l'écu*, angevins and mansois (that is, the coins of Nantes, Angers and Le Mans) and also English sterlings was temporarily permitted, but at a rate fixed by the royal treasury which, if not respected, was punishable first by a fine and then by confiscation. The prohibition of the coins of the barons of southern France and England was not the result simply of a desire to impose the primacy of those of the king but also of the need to increase the supply of white metal to the royal mints. We should not forget that, for most of the Middle Ages, Christendom suffered from a degree of monetary famine caused primarily by a shortage of white metal, due to the more or less rapid exhaustion, and small number, of the mines.

The principal monetary reforms introduced by Louis IX in the *ordonnance* of 24 July 1266, the full text of which, sadly, does not survive, are:

1 the resumption of the minting of the parisis;
2 the introduction of the gros tournois;
3 the introduction of the gold écu.

The last two measures show France, rather belatedly, especially compared with the great mercantile towns of Italy, adopting in response to the growth of trade the two most important monetary measures of the thirteenth century, that is, the creation of silver coins of high value and a return to the minting of gold. The decision to mint the gros tournois was the more important. This coin of high value, though less than that of gold, remained too valuable for the commercial activity of most parts of the West. However, it was well suited to the growth of French trade during what has been called, as I have already noted, 'the commercial revolution of the thirteenth century'. The success of the gros tournois was assured by the ban on its minting by the barons. Its value was approximately equivalent to that of twelve deniers tournois. It came to be called the 'gros of St Louis', whose reign, as is well known, became almost mythic by the fourteenth century in French memory ('the good times of Monseigneur Saint Louis'); it was also known as the 'gros aux deux *o* ronds' ('gros with the two round *o*s'), because the words *ludovicus* and *turonus* both had *o*s bigger than the other letters. The gros of St Louis was for a long time more highly prized than the others and it even withstood the monetary mutations of the late thirteenth and fourteenth centuries. The gold écu, on the other hand, was probably premature and it failed.

St Louis did not innovate as regards the administration of the royal treasury. He continued to rely on a post created in the twelfth century, that of royal treasurer, and on moneychangers called treasurers, created by Louis VII, and he also continued the latter's policy of entrusting the royal treasury to the Parisian house of the order of the Temple. We see once again the role played in this period by the great religious orders in the financial management of what we would call heads of state. The order of Cluny had administered the revenues and finances of the pontifical curia at the beginning of the twelfth century; the order of the Temple did the same for the French monarchy between the mid-twelfth century and 1295. The royal treasury was then withdrawn from the Temple to be placed in the Louvre, and later in the royal palace of the Cité which was rebuilt at the beginning of the fourteenth century.

The official responsible for financial matters in each of the divisions of the kingdom called *bailliages* (bailiwicks) was the *bailli*. He collected the taxes on land transfers (*droits de mutations*), redemptions of hospitality rights (*droits de gîte*), rents in kind from the communes, the royal taxes, called the regalia, stamp duty on documents marked with the royal seal (*droits de sceau*), the taxes paid by the Jews and the revenues from the forests until the creation of a special department of 'waters and forests' (*eaux et fôrets*) in 1287. From 1238, the *bailli* was responsible for the royal expenditure on pensions assigned by the king against the revenues of his *bailliage* (*fiefs et aumônes*) and on works, that is the building and repair of the castles, *hôtels*, houses, barns, prisons, mills, roads and bridges belonging to the king. The oldest document assessing royal wealth, and more particularly that of the royal demesne, chief financial resource of the sovereign, is a text of the provost of the church of Lausanne in 1222. It estimates the fortune of Philip Augustus at the start of his reign as an income of 19,000 livres per month (or 228,000 livres a year) left by his father Louis VII, whereas he himself was able to leave his son, the future Louis VIII, a daily income of 1,200 livres parisis, that is, an annual income of 438,000 livres parisis. These revenues made the monarchy the richest institution, after the Church, in the kingdom of France at the beginning of the thirteenth century. During that century, the king of France received a tax on merchandise sold in the markets and fairs called *tonlieu*. He also received innumerable tolls on travellers, their merchandise, their vehicles and their draught animals. These were collected at the entry to roads and ports and on bridges and waterways. A payment for the right to exercise a trade, the *hauban*, had to be made to the king in kind and in money. The king collected a tax called *seigniorage* on minting, which was assured either by melting down ingots or by re-minting used coins. He also received a tax for the use of the weights and measures used as benchmarks. He inherited from foreigners and bastards and levied taxes on Jewish usurers. Under the heading of *forêt*, that essential part of the royal demesne, the king drew a significant income from the felling of woods, from fishing and from the installation of dams and mills. If he was short of money, he could impose forced loans, especially on the towns. The expenses of the royal household were largely met from the income from stamp duty. The king's income thus came both as landowner and as sovereign. As the taxpayers made their payments in coin of the realm, the cashiers of the royal treasury had to know exactly how these related to the livre of account. This meant that they needed to have in front of them valuation (*avaluement*) tables for the coins which indicated the daily variations in their relationship to the livre of account and its subdivisions, whether in parisis or in tournois. The auditing of the royal accounts was not organized until the beginning of the fourteenth century, as we have seen, with the creation of the Chambre aux deniers which in 1320 became the Chambre des comptes. In the thirteenth century, the royal officials and farmers had to bring the money to the Treasury and present their accounts three times a year, on the feast of St Remigius (1 October), subsequently All Saints' Day (1 November), at Candlemas (2 February) and on Ascension Day (Thursday following Rogation Sunday, that is, the fifth Sunday after Easter), or rather in the week after these feasts.

The Capetian monarchy was thus fairly quick to organize its finances, and in particular its system of accounts. However, very few of the royal accounts survive, especially for the earlier period, only three rolls for 1202–3, which their editors, Ferdinand Lot and Robert Fawtier, called the monarchy's first budget.[3] It emerges that the total receipts of the monarchy came to 197,042 livres 12 sous, and its expenses to 95,445 livres. St Louis, who had added to the royal demesne by the acquisition of the Mâconnais in 1240, and who exercised great care in the administration of the woods and forests, which provided a quarter of the income from the demesne, insisted on the greatest possible accuracy in the accounts for these revenues. Those for 1234, 1238 and 1248 survive; that of the *prévôts* and *baillis* for Ascension Day 1248 was regarded as a masterpiece of presentation and taken as a model for a long time to come. The reign of St Louis bears out, therefore, Marc Bompaire's observation that 'money participated in the genesis of the modern state as a favoured instrument of prestige, a unifying factor and also as a source of revenue.' He recalls that, alongside this political aspect, a 'monetarization' of the economy also promoted the diffusion and importance of money. The Brazilian historian João Bernardo, in his monumental study,[4] argues that the spread of money during the long European thirteenth century was primarily linked to the transition from the personal seigneurial family to an artificial and impersonal state family. Money was thus, he believed, an agent in bringing about social transformations.

Far from such considerations, St Louis, like every Christian of his day, was concerned above all for his salvation and, as king, for that of his subjects too. His efforts to provide his country with good money sprang essentially from his desire to make justice prevail in commercial activities. He probably knew and remembered Isidore of Seville's definition of coinage: *moneta* comes from *monere*, 'to warn', because it warns against any sort of fraud in the metal or the weight. It was a battle against 'bad' money, money that was false, *falsa*, or falsified, *defraudata*, a striving for 'good' money, that was 'sound and true'. Thanks to this money, which he received in ever larger quantities, the king could fulfil one of his wishes which, as we will see, assumed an even more important place in the Christian religion in the thirteenth century, that is, charity. The king was a great distributor of alms, and though some of these handouts were in kind, others were in money. This is yet another sphere in which we can observe the increase in the circulation of coin in the thirteenth century.

The Hanse, an original institution

The Hanse was an institution which, though never a state, became from the twelfth century a great Christian, economic, social and political power, which brought the north and north-east of Christendom into the commercial revolution of the thirteenth century. This organization took shape with the foundation, in 1185, of the town of Lübeck, a western port that looked east. The town quickly became, and remained, the head of the Hanse, which was an association of the merchants of the principal trading towns of this region. They expanded their activities, taking over the trade of the Flemings and of certain German merchants, in particular the many and active merchants of Cologne. In fact, a first association of German merchants had been formed in the twelfth century, in the Swedish island of Gotland. Its principal town, Visby, was a double town, in which associations of German and Scandinavian merchants coexisted in close cooperation. It was a rival to Lübeck and, in the thirteenth century, tended to assume the direction and protection of Germans trading in Russia. Every year they deposited at Visby the treasure chest of the establishment founded in Novgorod. By the end of the twelfth century, however, Lübeck had made its superiority over Visby felt, as over all the other German towns.

For the Hanse, we have statistical information from the thirteenth century, thanks to the registers of debts introduced in several cities, including Hamburg, Lübeck and Riga. Of the sectors for which we have figures, it was only in England that its role was minor. The Hanseatics were able to impose on their partners a system for the settlement of debts that was extremely favourable to them, a sign of the growing importance of credit in long-distance trade in the thirteenth century. They also received a payment for the rescue of sailors and merchants threatened with shipwreck. Most important of all, they were able to achieve significant reductions in customs tariffs, to fix in minute detail the taxes to be paid and to win assurances that these taxes would not be increased and that no others would be imposed. This was the case, for example, with the tariff granted to the Hanseatics in

1252 by the Countess of Flanders. The use of credit, usually copied from the practices of the Italians, who were ahead in this aspect of money, spread widely throughout the Hanseatic trading area in the thirteenth century. It was regulated and, towards the end of the thirteenth century, the towns introduced registers of debts which provided the operations with an official guarantee. However, the increased circulation of money due to Hanseatic trading activities was limited in the eastern part of this area by the persistence of barter and 'fur-money', marten being the unit of currency. The introduction of metal coins failed in Pskov and Novgorod, where all sales on credit were forbidden at the end of the thirteenth century. With regard to money, the Hanseatics had some successes and some failures. Among the former was the precocious acquisition of minting rights by the towns, with the exception of certain Westphalian and Saxon towns where the bishops retained this right. The big failure was their inability to reduce the number of currencies circulating in the vast Hanseatic region, which put obstacles in the way of trade and added extra costs due to the exchange. There were, for example, marks of Lübeck, of Pomerania, of Prussia and of Riga, and also thalers of Brandenburg in the east and Rhineland guilders in the west. The most widespread moneys of account were the Lübeck mark, the Flemish pound of groschen and, to a lesser extent, the English pound sterling. The Hanseatics were deeply attached to silver coins and endeavoured to prevent the spread of gold coins in their region from the second half of the thirteenth century. The history of the Hanse shows how, in the Middle Ages, money gave rise to and accompanied the creation of some original economic and political entities.

7

Lending, Debt and Usury

The greater need for money experienced by most people in the West from the twelfth century came up against the problem of the shortfall in the quantity of money in circulation and, worse, that of the inadequacy of the pecuniary resources of medieval people. Amongst the most heavily indebted were certainly the peasantry. The sale of their produce, itself generally of low value, was restricted to local or regional markets, and it brought them very little cash until the spread, especially from the thirteenth century, of 'industrial' crops such as woad and hemp and the development of tools. The latter explains the increasing importance of the smith, who, as surnames began to appear, in the thirteenth century, provided numerous patronymics, including smith in English, *favre*, *fèvre* and *lefèvre* in French and *schmitt* or *schmidt* in German, not counting the languages which have today become dialects, like Breton, where smiths abounded under their Celtic name of *le goff*.

Lending at interest between Jews and Christians

Without dwelling on peasant indebtedness, which is difficult to study in detail, we should note that a large number of peasants, for example in the eastern Pyrenees, got into debt to Jewish moneylenders. In fact, the increase in the demand for money made the fortunes of the Jews, though often on a far smaller scale than was rumoured. Until the thirteenth century, in the context of the limited needs of that period, the main moneylenders had been monastic institutions. Later, when the use of money spread to the towns, the Jews played a major role because, according to the biblical and Old Testament sources quoted above, lending at interest was forbidden both between Christians and between Jews, at least in theory, though it was permitted between Jews and Christians. The Jews, excluded from agriculture, found a source of income in certain urban trades such as medicine, which they could supplement by lending to poor Christians in the towns. The Jews play only a minor role in this book because, in the parts of Europe where the circulation of money was most active, they were replaced at a fairly early stage, in the twelfth and even more the thirteenth century, by Christians, and then expelled from much of Europe – from England in 1290, from France first in 1306, then definitively in 1394. We see that the image of the Jew as money-grubber was based less on reality, though small-scale Jewish moneylenders did exist, than on a fantasy prefiguring the anti-Semitism of the nineteenth century.[1]

Lending was naturally accompanied by the payment of interest on the part of the borrowers. Yet the Church forbade Christian creditors from taking interest from Christian debtors. The texts most commonly invoked were: *Mutuum date, nihil inde sperantes* (Lend, expecting nothing in return: Luke, 6.35); 'Take thou no usury of [thy brother], or increase' (Leviticus, 25.36); and 'Unto a stranger thou mayest lend upon usury; but unto thy brother thou shalt not lend upon usury' (Deuteronomy 23.20). The Decree of Gratian, which was in the twelfth century the basis of canon law, ran: *Quicquid ultra sortem exigitur usura est* (Whatever is demanded above the capital is usury).

The canon law code best expresses the Church's attitude to usury in the thirteenth century: usury was everything that was demanded in exchange for a loan beyond the loan itself; to take usury was a sin forbidden by both the Old and the New Testaments; the mere hope of something in return beyond what had been lent was a sin; usurious gains should be restored in full to their rightful owner; higher prices for a sale on credit were implicit usury.

The main consequences of this doctrine were:

1 Usury was a form of the mortal sin of avarice (*avaritia*). The other mortal sin of *avaritia* was trafficking in spiritual

goods, called simony, which was in rapid decline since the Gregorian Reform introduced in the late eleventh and twelfth centuries.

2 Usury was a theft, the theft of time, which belonged solely to God, because it made money out of the time that elapsed between the loan and its repayment. It gave rise to a new type of time, usurious time. I should stress here that money profoundly altered the conception and practice of time in the Middle Ages, when, as Jean Ibanès has shown, many times coexisted.[2] We see once again the extent to which the increase in the circulation of money altered the principal structures of life, of morality and of religion in the Middle Ages.

3 Usury was a sin against justice, as was emphasized, in particular, by St Thomas Aquinas;[3] the thirteenth century was the century par excellence of justice, which was the eminent virtue of kings, as was shown, in his behaviour as a man and as a king, by St Louis IX of France.

The usurer doomed

The thirteenth century added to the diabolical nature of money a new dimension, which the great scholastic writers borrowed from Aristotle, himself a major intellectual discovery of that century. 'Money', said Thomas Aquinas, after Aristotle, 'does not reproduce itself' (*nummus non parit nummos*). Thus usury was also a sin against nature, which was now, in the eyes of the scholastic theologians, a divine creation.

What, then, was the inexorable fate of the usurer? There was no salvation for him, as we see from the sculptures in which a purse full of money hanging round his neck drags him down to Hell. Pope Leo I the Great had said in the fifth century: 'Usurious profit from money is the death of the soul' (*Fenus pecuniae, funus est animae*). In 1179, the Third Lateran Council declared that usurers were foreigners in Christian towns and that they should be refused Christian burial.

Usury was death.

Many thirteenth-century texts describe the horrible death of the usurer. This is what one anonymous manuscript of the period said:

> Usurers sin against nature by seeking to breed money from money, like a male horse from a male horse or a male mule from a male mule. What is more, usurers are thieves because they sell time, which does not belong to them, and to sell something that is not your own against the wishes of its owner is theft. Further, as all they sell is waiting for money, that is, time, they are selling days and nights. But day is the time of light and night is the time of repose. So, they sell light and repose. It would not be just, therefore, for them to have eternal light and eternal repose.[4]

Another professional category experienced a similar evolution at the same period, that is, the 'new intellectuals'. These were men who, outside the monastic schools and cathedrals, taught students from whom they received payment, the *collecta*. Among those who denounced them was St Bernard. He castigated them as 'sellers and merchants of words' because they sold knowledge, which, like time, belonged only to God. In the thirteenth century, these intellectuals organized themselves into universities which, by a system of prebends, provided them not only with the bare necessities but with, on the whole, a comfortable living, though this is not to say that no poor university teachers existed. At all events, the new discourse of these new intellectuals was linked in a particular way to money, which was insinuating itself into every human activity, both traditional and new.

In one of the oldest of the manuals (*summa*) for confessors written at the beginning of the thirteenth century, that of Thomas of Chobham, an Englishman trained in the University of Paris, we find the following observation: 'The usurer wishes to acquire a profit without any labour, even while asleep; which goes against the precept of the Lord, who said: "In the sweat of thy face shalt thou eat bread"' (Genesis, 3.19). Here we see a new theme, which made a major contribution to the flowering of the thirteenth century, and which coincided with the rise of money, the valorization of work.

For most of the thirteenth century, the only way in which the usurer could avoid going to Hell was to restore what he had gained through taking interest, that is, usury. The best restitution was that performed by the usurer before his death, but he could also save himself after death by including the restitution in his will. In this case, his responsibility and his risk of going to Hell were transmitted to his heirs or the executors of his will. Here is a story from the *Tabula exemplorum*, dating from the end of the thirteenth century:

> On his death, a usurer willed all his property to three executors, charging them on oath to make full restitution. He had asked them what they feared most in the world. The first replied, 'Poverty', the second, 'Leprosy' and the third, 'St Anthony's fire' [ergotism] ... but after his death the greedy legatees took all the dead man's possessions for themselves. Very soon after, they were afflicted by everything the dead man had called down by imprecations, poverty, leprosy and the Holy Fire.

We have very few documents to inform us about the realities of the restitution of usurious sums in the Middle Ages. Some historians, who do not accept the total dominance of religion over the people of this period, believe it must have been very limited. I myself am of the opinion that, on the contrary, the hold of the Church over minds and the fear of Hell in the thirteenth century was such that it must have led to many instances of restitution; and in fact some churchmen wrote treatises *De restitutionibus* to tell people how to do this.

In any case, the act of restitution was regarded in the Middle Ages as particularly painful to perform. There is unexpected evidence of this in a declaration of St Louis reported by Joinville:

> He said that it was an evil thing to take what belonged to another because to give it back was so hard that even to say the word 'restore' grates in the throat because of the 'r's in it, which stand for the rakes of the devil, who will always drag back those who want to restore the property of another. And the devil does this very skilfully because, with the great usurers and the great thieves, he stirs them up in such a way that he makes them give to God that which they ought to restore.

The thirteenth-century Church was not content with dooming the usurer to Hell. It also reminded him of the scorn and the reproaches of men. A famous early thirteenth-century preacher, Jacques de Vitry, told this story:

> A preacher wanted to demonstrate to everyone that the usurer's trade was so shameful that no one dared admit to it, so he said in

> his sermon, 'I want to give you absolution according to your activities and your trades. All the blacksmiths stand up!' and they stood up. Having given them absolution, he said, 'All the furriers stand up!' and they stood up, and so on as he named the different artisans in turn, and they stood up. Finally, he shouted, 'All the usurers stand up to receive absolution!' The usurers were more numerous than the other trades but, out of shame, they hid. To laughter and catcalls they withdrew in confusion.

In this medieval world, where symbolism reigned supreme, as Michel Pastoureau has shown, and where the animals provided a rich store of models of evil, the usurer was frequently likened to a rapacious lion or a perfidious fox or a thieving and voracious wolf. Extending the metaphor, the preachers and writers of the Middle Ages often presented the usurer as an animal shedding its coat at the time of its death, its coat being the riches it had stolen. The animal most often employed symbolically to describe the usurer was the spider, and medieval imagery exploited this comparison also to infer the practice attributed to usurers of persisting in ignominy with their heirs. This is how Jacques de Vitry describes the funeral of a usurer spider:

> I heard tell of a knight, that he met a group of monks who were on their way to bury the corpse of a usurer. He said to them, 'I will let you have the corpse of my spider and let the Devil have his soul. But *I* will have the spider's web, that is to say, all its money.' It is quite right to compare usurers to spiders, who eviscerate themselves in order to trap flies, and who sacrifice to the devil not only themselves but also their sons, dragging them into the fire of greed... this process is perpetuated with their heirs. In fact, some of them, even before the birth of their sons, assign them money so they will multiply by usury and thus their sons are born hairy like Esau and extremely rich. On their death they leave their money to their sons, who then begin to wage a new war on God.

It is well known that the medieval Church, as Georges Dumézil has shown, ordered society into three sorts of men: those who prayed, those who fought and those who worked. Jacques de Vitry adds a fourth category. 'The Devil', he says, 'created a fourth sort of man, the usurers. They do not share in the work of men and they will not be punished with men but with the demons. Because the quantity of money they receive from usury will be matched by the quantity of wood sent to Hell to burn them.'

Sometimes God did not wait for death to deliver the usurer to the devil and to Hell. The preachers tell that many usurers, with the approach of death, lost the power of speech and so were unable to confess. Worse still, many died a sudden death, the worst death of all for a medieval Christian because it left the usurer no time to confess his sin.

In the middle of the thirteenth century a Dominican from the Convent of the Preachers in Lyon, Stephen of Bourbon, told a story which seems to have circulated widely and enjoyed huge popularity:

> It happened in Dijon about the year of Our Lord 1240 that a usurer wanted to celebrate his wedding with great pomp. To the sound of music he was conducted to the parish church of the Blessed Virgin. He stood beneath the church porch so that his fiancée could state her consent and the marriage be ratified according to custom by the ritual words, before the marriage was crowned by the celebration of the mass and other rites inside the church.[5] As the bride and the groom, full of joy, were about to enter the church, a stone usurer carved above the porch in the act of being carried off by the Devil to Hell, fell, with his purse, onto the head of the living usurer who was about to be married, and struck him dead. The nuptials turned to grief, rejoicing to sadness.

Here we have a notable example of the remarkably active role the Middle Ages could attribute to the image, and in particular to sculpture. Art was enlisted to serve in the battle against the improper use of money.

A whole 'thriller' literary genre was devoted to the lives and deaths of medieval usurers. Usurious money was one of the deadliest weapons of the age. Here is one of the best of these stories, as told by Stephen of Bourbon:

> I have heard tell of a usurer who was seriously ill and who did not wish to make any restitution at all but who nevertheless ordered that his barn full of grain be distributed to the poor. When the servants came to collect the grain they found it had turned into snakes. When he learned of this, the contrite usurer made full restitution and ordered that his corpse be thrown naked into the

middle of the snakes so that it would be devoured by the snakes here below to avoid his soul being devoured in the hereafter. This was done. The snakes devoured his body, leaving behind only whitened bones. Some add that when they had done their work, the snakes disappeared and all that remained were the bare white bones in the light of day.

The gradual justification of lending at interest

I want now to show how lending at interest, the basis of usury, was gradually, and on certain conditions, rehabilitated during the course of the thirteenth and even more the fourteenth and fifteenth centuries. This rehabilitation was justified by the desire of the usurers to remain good Christians and of some Churchmen to save even the worst sinners by introducing changes into conceptions of the life of man and of society that they believed were made necessary by new developments; the chief of these was the spread of money. In a society now subject to monetary practices, the fundamental values dictating human and social existence in thirteenth-century Christendom were changing; I believe we can detect here what I have elsewhere called 'a descent to earth of the values of heaven'.[6] The first of these values to prevail in the thirteenth century was justice. Above it, however, was *caritas*, that is, love. We will see how the spread of money could be reconciled with the requirement for *caritas*, which relates more to a gift economy, according to a different conception from that of Marcel Mauss, author of the famous *The Gift: Forms and Functions of Exchange in Archaic Societies* (first published 1923–4, first English edition 1954). Added to which were the effects of the valorization of work, which introduced a particular dimension into the use and spread of money, especially through the importance of the new wage earners. I will content myself here with noting what seems to me to be the first means adopted by medieval society, and in particular the Church, in order to ensure that the usurer was not inevitably and in all circumstances doomed to Hell.

I tried to explain some years ago how, in the second half of the twelfth century, there appeared in the West, with regard to the hereafter, major preoccupation of all Christians, an intermediate hereafter, that is, Purgatory.[7] For a period of time proportionate to the number and gravity of their sins at the time of their death, Christians suffered a certain number of tortures of infernal character in this intermediate hereafter, but escaped everlasting Hell. When they had sufficiently expiated their sins in Purgatory or, at the latest, when the Last Judgement left only the prospect of eternal Paradise or Hell, some usurers whose case was not irremediable could escape Hell and, like the other artisans referred to by Jacques de Vitry, be received in Paradise. The first known rescue of a usurer by Purgatory is found in a treatise of the German Cistercian Caesarius of Heisterbach, the *Dialogus magnus visionum ac miraculorum* of around 1220, which tells the story of a usurer of Liege:

> A usurer of Liege died not long ago. The bishop had him thrown out of the cemetery. His wife went to the apostolic see to beg for him to be buried in holy ground. The pope refused. She then pleaded for her husband as follows: 'I have heard tell, my Lord, that man and wife are one and that according to the Apostle the unbelieving man can be saved by the believing woman. What my husband forgot to do, I, who am part of his flesh, will gladly do in his place. I am ready to become a recluse for him and to atone to God for his sins.' Giving in to the prayers of the cardinals, the pope had the dead man returned to the cemetery. His wife took up residence next to his tomb, shut herself up as a recluse, and strove day and night to appease God for the salvation of his soul by alms, fasts, prayers and vigils. After seven years, her husband appeared to her robed in black and thanked her: 'May God reward you, because thanks to your hardships I have been removed from the depths of Hell and the most terrible punishments. If you perform such services for me for another seven years, I will be freed altogether.' This she did. He appeared to her again after seven years, but this time robed in white and with a joyful air: 'Thanks be to God and to you because today I have been liberated.'

Caesarius goes on to explain that the intermediate sojourn of the usurer of Liege between his death and the liberation of his soul by his wife was Purgatory. This is the oldest known account of a usurer saved by this method. Purgatory was not, of course, created for the purpose of saving usurers from Hell, but, as part of a much broader and revised conception of the hereafter, it remains the case that the story of the usurer of Liege makes a connection between Purgatory and money. We can now say, with Nicole Bériou, that the spirit of lucre in Christendom was situated 'between vice and virtue'.[8]

Purgatory was not, of course, the main way in which usurers were saved from Hell in the thirteenth century. Gradually, beginning in the thirteenth century and continuing until the end of the fifteenth, there was a growing tendency to define circumstances that would allow what the medieval Church called usury, or usurious loans. Usury, we should remember, meant lending at interest, in particular the taking of interest on money loaned. One consequence of the rapid increase in the diffusion and use of money was a huge increase in indebtedness in every social class of western society in the thirteenth century. This indebtedness, as noted above, primarily affected the peasants, who had not previously handled or possessed money on any significant scale. However, in what Marc Bloch called the second stage of feudalism, they were forced to make use of coin, due, in large part, to the commutation into money rents of many renders in kind. In some regions, the countryside was fertile territory for Jewish moneylenders, who grew rich, but who were increasingly supplanted by Christians. More generally, those who lent money in the countryside were Christians from the towns or rich Christian peasants who found lending to their poor and indebted fellows a way of increasing their incomes, thus consolidating the existence of a prosperous peasant class.

Broadly speaking, the changes in ecclesiastical and princely regulation and in attitudes hostile to the use of money were accompanied by similar changes with regard to merchants. In fact, by the eleventh century, in particular through the use of the Peace of God or the Peace of the prince, merchants were protected by the Church and by the lords, who then needed to justify this attitude. Two main reasons were put forward. The first was utility. Medieval Christianity had never clearly distinguished between the good, or even the beautiful, and the useful. The increase in the living standards and basic needs of the medieval population, especially in the towns, gradually justified from the twelfth century the activities of the peasants by their utility: they provided all or certain categories of Christians with products they either had need of or craved. Among the former were the cereals from which bread, the basic foodstuff of the West, was made, though we should not forget sea and rock salt; among the latter, we may note those which had the greatest success: spices, furs and silks.

Labour and risk

The second main justification for mercantile profit was as a reward for labour. By the Early Middle Ages, Christianity had already long despised work as the consequence of original sin. The third category in the tripartite division of society, the *laboratores*, those who worked, meant essentially the peasants, who came bottom in the feudal social scale. The attitude of the monks, the principal diffusers of values in the Early Middle Ages, was ambiguous. The Rule of St Benedict in particular made manual labour obligatory, but this was primarily as a form of contrition and many monks abandoned it to the lay brethren. From the twelfth century, however, work was the beneficiary of a remarkable promotion in the value system and in social prestige, which took place more or less in parallel with the revalorization of the person and of the role of women, encouraged by the huge expansion of the Marian cult. Man had previously been presented as a creature punished and suffering like Job. He was now, as the Church recalled in commenting on Genesis, a creature made by God in his image during the Creation, the first 'work' in history performed by a God who, exhausted, had 'rested on the seventh day'. The man who worked thus became a co-worker with God in his construction of a world which struggled to live up to the expectations of its Creator.

In addition to these two essential values for the rehabilitation of the merchant, and soon of the usurer, the thirteenth-century scholastics developed principles which made it legitimate for a moneylender to ask for and receive a financial reward linked to the amount of money he had lent, that is, interest.

The first justification to spread from the merchant to the lender was the risk the latter incurred. Here I differ from Alain Guerreau, although I am generally in agreement with his wise views on medieval society. Sylvain Piron has shown how the term *resicum* appeared among Mediterranean notaries and merchants in the late twelfth and early thirteenth centuries. It was through the intermediary of the Catalan Dominican Raymond de Penafort, who used it in connection with the 'maritime loan' (*foenus nauticum*), that this word appeared in the vocabulary and thinking of the scholastic theologians.[9] Medieval people long retained a special fear of the sea. Travel by road might be threatened by lords greedy for taxes on traffic, or even more by bandits, especially when the route ran through a forest, but the most dangerous place of all according to paintings and ex-votos was the sea. When it did not threaten the merchant's life, it threatened the safe delivery of his merchandise, and the frequency of shipwrecks, even more than of pirates, justified him, in compensation for the risk, in taking interest, usury, the *damnum emergens*, *periculum sortis*, *ratio incertitudinis*.

Another justification for charging interest was the renunciation for the duration of the loan of any direct profit from the money loaned (*lucrum cessans*), together with recompense for the work by which this money had been produced (*stipendium laboris*).

Usury continued to be widely and fiercely condemned in the thirteenth century, and the Hell awaiting the usurer was evoked, even where lending at interest, hence usury, was tolerated. Nevertheless, it was slowly and painfully accepted as legitimate because of its encounter with another great principle, the notion of justice. In this context, justice essentially meant a reasonable rate of interest. This rate remained, nevertheless, at a level that seems very high to us, around 20 per cent. Above all, however, lending at interest, in particular in the eyes of the Church, was balanced in the second half of thirteenth century between the traditional desire to condemn it and prohibit its use and the new trend to justify it within certain limits. We see this in the treatise *De usuris*, written at the end of the thirteenth century by a Dominican who was probably a disciple of Albert the Great, Giles de Lessines, who says: 'Doubt and risk cannot erase the spirit of gain, that is, excuse usury, but when there is uncertainty and no calculation, doubt and risk can be equated with justice.'

A number of problems surrounding money and usury were the subject of discussion at *quodlibets* at the University of Paris in the late thirteenth century, that is, disputations at which any topic could be raised, especially those touching on matters of current concern. Between 1265 and 1290, the most famous master of the day at the University of Paris, Henry of Ghent, debated life rents and perpetual rents with other masters, Matthew of Aquasparta, Gervase of Mont-Saint-Eloi, Richard of Middleton and Godfrey of Fontaines. The debate turned on the question of whether or not this was usury. Opinion was divided, but the discussion shows that, starting from the problem of usury and all it involved, the ethics of the new economic practices based on the use of money and valuation in money had entered the domain of the theologians.[10]

If these problems preoccupied the theologians, they were a much greater cause for concern to the merchants and moneylenders who, as good Christians, wished to be spared Hell but wished also to grow rich. I have described their quandary elsewhere, in a book with the title *Your Money or Your Life*.

As a further illustration of this change in the attitude to money, I will quote an example from the fine book of Chiara Frugoni, *L'Affare migliore di Enrico: Giotto e la cappella Scrovegni*. Frugoni discusses the remarkable turnaround in the image of the Scrovegni family represented by the construction of the chapel in Padua decorated by the frescoes commissioned by Enrico Scrovegni from Giotto at the beginning of the fourteenth century. The Scrovegni family was a Paduan example of the new wealth of the long thirteenth century. Dante had put the father among the usurers of Hell. His son Enrico continued and even expanded his father's business but expressed his *caritas* by building this chapel, dedicated to Santa Maria della Carità and to the poor, where Giotto altered the traditional order in which the virtues and vices were represented. Enrico, who died in exile in Venice for purely political reasons, has left behind the image of a great benefactor; this usurer was destined for Paradise.

In the Church, those who were most alert to the problems caused by money were the new mendicant orders, the Dominicans and especially the Franciscans. The terms of the debate shifted and it became, in new forms, one of the great issues of the Middle Ages. Just as there had been, in the case of food, the great battle between Carnival and Lent, so, in the case of money, there was a great battle between wealth and poverty.

8

A New Wealth and a New Poverty

However, this battle was between a new wealth and a new poverty. It was the thirteenth century which saw what I have termed 'the descent to earth of the values of heaven'. The wealth was new. It was no longer that of land, of the lords and of the monasteries; it was that of the burgesses, of the merchants and of those who were called usurers and who would soon become bankers. It was wealth expressed in monetary value, whether it was real money or money of account.

It remains the case that this new wealth had more social significance than it had purely economic importance. The new rich would take their place among the powerful of Christian society because, faced with their new wealth, a new poverty would now rank their activities not with greed and the vices but with *caritas*, of which I have already spoken, and the virtues. All through the thirteenth century, money oscillated, as Nicole Bériou has shown, between vice and virtue. In his book of 1978, the American historian Lester K. Little explained how religious poverty and the profit economy had come to coexist in medieval Europe.[1] Money had long ago insinuated itself into the Christian imaginary. At the beginning of the twelfth century, the French monk Geoffroy of Vendôme had compared the consecrated host to a perfectly struck coin, its roundness recalling the roundness of a coin, just as the capacity of the host to be equivalent to salvation recalled the capacity of the coin to represent a value. St

Augustine had already, in the time of the fathers of the church, made Christ the first merchant, whose sacrifice had redeemed humanity – he was 'the celestial merchant'. But in the twelfth and even more the thirteenth century, it was a new wealth that spread through Christendom.

The new poor

This new wealth was contrasted with a new poverty. This poverty was no longer a consequence of original sin, nor was it the poverty of Job; it was a valorized poverty, in line with the changed image of Jesus in Christian spirituality. Jesus was increasingly less what he had been in the first centuries of Christianity, the man-God who had risen from the dead, the great Victor over death. He had become the man-God who had given humans the model of poverty symbolized by nakedness. In all the movements which attempted, after the year 1000, to revive primitive Christianity and inspire a return to the apostles, the strongest inspiration had been that urging reform and renewal through a return to the sources, for people to 'follow naked the naked Christ'. Just as the new wealth resulted from work, the new poverty resulted from an effort, from a choice; it was a voluntary poverty, and we cannot truly understand how money established itself in medieval society if we do not distinguish between these two types of poverty, one suffered, the other voluntary.[2]

Frantisek Graus has shown that the countryside had its poor in the Early Middle Ages, but the place where poverty was greatest and most visible in the Middle Ages was the town. It was to be expected, therefore, that the battle against the new poverty would primarily be fought by the new religious orders who, unlike their monkish predecessors, settled in the towns, in particular the Franciscans.

In every sense of the word, Francis of Assisi asserted himself through the rejection of money.[3] He disowned his merchant father, he went naked like Jesus, he lived in poverty, he preached in poverty. And then, paradoxically, the denigrators of the new wealth, in seeking to promote the new poverty, achieved an ambiguous, even opposite, result. As Little pointed out, in 1261 the archbishop of Pisa, preaching in the church of the Franciscans, made Francis of Assisi the patron and protector of merchants. The

Italian historian Giacomo Todeschini has gone further. He believes that Francis had by the end of his life reconciled poverty and the urban culture characterized by money which had developed in northern and central Italy. During the course of the thirteenth century, says Todeschini, the Franciscans continued to define and justify a Franciscan wealth which led them 'from voluntary poverty to the market society'. Todeschini was primarily basing himself on the treatise of the Languedocian Franciscan Peter John Olivi (1248–1298), the *De contractibus*, written around 1295.[4]

More interesting perhaps, because more firmly anchored in daily life, is a register of the convent of the Friars Minor of Padua and Vicenza (1263–1302), which notes the deposits, sales, purchases and other contracts made by the Franciscans of these two towns. It contains more references to loans in money than to acquisitions and exchanges of land; the Friars Minor, it would appear, even from within poverty, though mostly through the intermediary of laymen acting in their name, were better integrated into the new monetary economy than into the old rural economy.[5]

Above all, the mendicant orders, and principally the Franciscans, had created from voluntary poverty the spiritual and social means to attract the new wealth towards the poor. It was largely under their influence that, in the thirteenth century, the Church and powerful laymen tried to combat the new wealth and promote the new poverty by special forms of what had always been one of the essential activities of, first, the Church and then of the Christians who had the means and the necessary social status: the works that we call charitable, but which in the Middle Ages were more often called mercies, the mercy of men having as its foundation the mercy of God. This mercy was most apparent in attention to the body, the body which was that of the suffering Christ and which would rise from the dead. The thirteenth century saw a massive and striking increase in hospital foundations and in their activities. These institutions, which had appeared in the Early Middle Ages and been put under the authority of the bishops, enjoyed a juridical autonomy which made it possible for them to receive gifts and legacies. The spread of money in the thirteenth century and the practice of a new charity could then operate in favour of the hospitals, and veritable religious orders devoted to their activities emerged. Two networks developed; on the one hand, there were the hospices, where the poor and pilgrims were given food and shelter for the night, on the other, the hospitals, where the sick, women in childbirth, orphans and abandoned children were received. The financial management of the hospitals was often entrusted to an administrator appointed by the bishop or the lay patron. As well as the initial and later donations, the hospitals received additional resources, either in kind (such as clothes and linen) or cash (collections and alms). The size and beauty of some of the hospitals remaining from the Late Middle Ages is an indication of the scale of the sums invested in them and of the amount of money spent on them. Having once been primarily associated with the roads, the hospitals came, between the twelfth and the fifteenth centuries, to be primarily associated with urban growth, as one can see in France, most notably at Angers, Beaune, Lille and Tonnerre. An increase in almsgiving in connection with the hospitals has been observed. The growth of charity was closely linked to the appearance of the new wealth and the new poverty, as the Franciscans knew them.

However, we should not exaggerate the role of the Franciscans or distort their motives or those of the Church. At the beginning of the thirteenth century, when the Church first canonized a merchant, St Homobonus of Cremona, it was explicitly stated that this was not because of his occupation but, on the contrary, because he had turned his back on it and devoted himself to voluntary poverty. St Francis himself never compromised on the matter of money; Peter John Olivi was a marginal Franciscan and the subject of much criticism after his death, while his *De contractibus* remained a unique treatise of its type. The most widely held attitude in the Church with regard to money, and usury in particular, at the end of the thirteenth century remained that of the *De usuris* of Giles of Lessines. This treatise, as we have seen, continued to condemn usury, even though some signs of tolerance are visible. What mattered in the sphere of money, as in all spheres in the thirteenth century, was moderation and the desire for justice. This was even clearer in the doctrine and practice of the 'just price', to which I will return.[6]

Price control

Famine was one of the greatest fears of medieval people, and cereal prices, which determined bread prices, were therefore strictly controlled by the municipal authorities. It seems, from the very incomplete figures at our disposal, that these prices rose steadily throughout the thirteenth century, although they fluctuated during the course of the year, according to the weather in particular, but also according to the greater or lesser abundance of the harvest. This is proof that the life of medieval men and women, and in particular their food consumption, was closely linked to nature, a dependence that was only slightly reduced by the spread of money both in general economic life and in daily life, a sign of the relatively slight impact of money on medieval activity.

Though the question of prices was in practice a matter for the producers, the sellers and the institutional regulators of markets, it was given careful consideration by the jurists and the theologians in the context of the debate about justice, that major preoccupation of the thirteenth century. From the juridical point of view, the canonists, who developed a specific law from the religious standpoint, seem to have followed the theories of the Romanists who had been reviving Roman law since the twelfth century. Nevertheless, the historians who have studied this problem in the Middle Ages, such as John Baldwin and Jean Ibanès, detect a transformation in thinking in the transition from Roman to canon law. They have noted this in particular in the work of the canonist Henry of Segusio, called Hostiensis, who died in 1270 and whose *Summa aurea*, written c.1250, strongly influenced the ideas and the actions of many thirteenth-century popes. Hostiensis, a doctor in both Roman and canon law, significantly changed the conception of price. The Romanists believed that the price was determined by the agreement between the contracting parties, that is, by an active negotiation which followed its own logic and was not subject to any external norm. The canonists developed the new thesis of a just price that existed of itself, independently of the agreement between the contracting parties, thus replacing an empirical law by a normative approach. John Baldwin has shown that the just price generally prevailed, concretely, in local markets in the central Middle Ages, and that it was characterized by its moderation, which brings it close to the generally sought-after ideal of justice. Yet, in reality, the merchants, especially those engaged in long-distance trade, what we would call exporters, tried to maximize their profits, which inclined them to engage in usurious practices. This provoked the suspicion, even condemnation, of the Church and even of lay institutions. Prices varied throughout the long thirteenth century, fluctuating, in the words of Nicole Bériou, 'between vice and virtue'.

Associations and companies

In the thirteenth century, the need to respond to an increased demand for money and to establish solidarity between craftsmen or merchants led to various forms of association, just as, in other spheres of life, there were confraternities and charities. An exceptional record, the *Livre des métiers* (*Book of Trades*) of the provost of Paris, Etienne Boileau, dating from the end of the reign of St Louis (c.1265), reveals the extreme fragmentation of craft manufacture into highly specialized trades, the secondary importance of money in the structure and functioning of these trades, where apprenticeship was often free and more dependent on social relationships than on financial possibilities, and the strict regulation of economic life. The spread of money encouraged the growth of writing and also of accounting, which led to the proliferation in the thirteenth century of manuals of arithmetic. The increasing sedentarization of merchants in this same period reduced the significance of fairs, although they remained important for exchange and monetary transactions until the end of the Middle Ages, as is shown by the rivalry between the fairs of Lyon and Geneva in the fifteenth century. This led to an increase in the number of contracts and associations by which merchants could extend their business networks and which involved the use of money, whether in the transfer of real money or in valuations in money of account.

One widespread form of association was the contract called the *commenda*, also called the *societas maris* in Genoa and the *collegantia* in Venice. In the *commenda*, the contracting parties joined together to share the risks and the profits, but otherwise the relations were those of lender and borrower.[7] There was a wider range of types of contract of association for trade on land, but they can be narrowed down to two basic types, the *compagnia* and the *societas terrae*. Unlike the contracts for sea trade, these were agreed for a fixed period of time, between one and four years.

Complex organizations, some more powerful than others, developed round certain merchants and certain families, which are often referred to as companies, though they were different from the organizations to which we give this name today. These companies, which first appeared in northern Italy, and also southern France, were given names which recalled their place of origin and which persisted even when their basis of operations had changed: the Cahorsins in France, the Lombards in Italy – the latter often from Asti[8] – and, in central Italy, the Sienese and the Florentines. In the second half of the long thirteenth century, these companies switched from the basic activity of trade to the more diversified, complex and speculative activities of true banks. These banks modernized their accounting and made it more efficient, in particular by the system of double-entry bookkeeping. The main technical innovation of the bankers was the slow spread, from the second half of the thirteenth century, of the bill of exchange, which I will discuss in more detail below.[9] The result was a money market which, as we will see, became very active in the fourteenth and fifteenth centuries and introduced a high volume of speculation into a large part of Christendom.

In addition to the numerous account books many merchants kept to facilitate their activities, they compiled and carefully preserved a 'secret book' containing the information most useful to them; these, according to Armando Sapori, are the documents with the highest survival rate of all this bookkeeping activity.

By the end of the long thirteenth century, that is, by the beginning of the fourteenth century, the use and the circulation of money had spread throughout most of Christendom, though unevenly; the Low Countries and the Hanseatic League, for example, had developed their trade but played almost no part in the development of banking. It is at this point that we see the first signs of difficulties due to the use and circulation of money. The most serious were the bank failures and the sudden changes in the value of coins, what are called monetary mutations. There was also, before the great revolts of the late fourteenth century, the oldest wave of urban strikes and uprisings in France in 1280, about which little is known; the role played in them by the new aspects of the use of monetary values is far from clear.

The difficulties experienced by the banks led some of them, and by no means the least, into bankruptcy. This was a world where indebtedness had increased and where individuals and companies had sometimes taken huge risks; above all, the banks had found themselves pressurized by the Holy See or by princes into making loans that remained unpaid for long periods, putting a serious strain on their reserves and causing some to fail. This was the case in 1294 with the Riccardi of Lucca, the Ammanati and the Chiarenti of Pistoia and, most notably, the Bonsignori of Siena in 1298. The Florentine companies, such as the Bardi, the Peruzzi and the Acciajuoli, ruined by the demands of the kings of England as they prepared for the Hundred Years War, and of the popes of Avignon as they built their superb palace, collapsed in a veritable crash in 1341.

9

From the Thirteenth to the Fourteenth Century: Money in Crisis

During the long thirteenth century, as we have seen, the increase in specie made it possible both to spend more and to buy more, while the increase in needs led to a much wider recourse to money. The rapid rise in expenditure began to provoke not only constant criticism from the Church but also interventions on the part of the nascent states. By the end of the twelfth century, John of Salisbury, one of Henry II's counsellors, in his political treatise, the *Policraticus*, had advised kings to regulate the use of money according to the needs of their subjects, but by adjusting the relationship between labour and necessity.[1] I have already discussed Philip the Fair's sumptuary *ordonnance* of 1294.

We know very little about other factors leading to an increased use of money, in particular the rise in the number and value of loans and consequently of indebtedness, for which the documentation is very poor. As we have seen, what pushed this indebtedness to a peak was the role of the princes, then in the process of building up their administrations and their states without yet having access to adequate financial means, and whose demands for loans it was impossible for the bankers to refuse.

Cahorsins, Lombards and moneychangers

In the early fourteenth century, these phenomena were still limited to a restricted number of persons from one part of Europe, that is, northern Italy. Some of these banker–moneylenders were for a while called Cahorsins, as they included men who had originally been based in Cahors, but by the second half of the thirteenth century they were usually called Lombards. Though Milan had become the main business centre by the end of the century, and Genoa and, above all, Venice had become linchpins in the trade in money between the Mediterranean and the East and the North Sea and the Low Countries, these Lombards had originated in historically less famous places, such as the town of Asti, in Piedmont. The Lombards were found more or less everywhere in western Europe. Their relations with the kings of France were complicated and turbulent, as the latter tried to take advantage of their financial assistance while at the same time defending their own power, asserted in the monetary sphere. Measures discriminating against the Lombards were introduced on several occasions under Philip the Fair, including arbitrary arrests. The king initiated various investigations into the Lombards, most notably in 1303–5 and 1309–11. Philip V (1316–22) and Charles IV (1322–8) demanded 'gifts' from them. As we have seen, many Sienese and Florentine companies were ruined by loans to the king of France that remained unpaid, and were bankrupted. The body blow came at the beginning of the reign of Philip VI (1328–50) when he was financing his preparations for the Hundred Years War.[2]

In England and the Low Countries, by contrast, the Lombards were generally better treated. David Kusman has studied the connections of Giovanni di Mirabello, a Piedmontese who settled in Brabant, where he became a great banker under the name of Van Haelen (c.1280–1333), and was ennobled and made a counsellor of the duke of Brabant.[3] This was in spite of the fact that he had been imprisoned for some months in 1318–19 by the municipality of Malines, after a complaint had been made against him by a private person, which shows the persistence of the ambivalent status of money at the beginning of the fourteenth century. Similarly, the Lombards were of crucial importance to the kings of England in the late thirteenth and early fourteenth centuries, with the company of the Malabaila and the Società dei Leopardi, both established in London.[4] In general, however, they were detested and reviled in most of Christendom, where money had not yet acquired an aura of respectability and where everyone who was in debt, to whatever extent and whatever their social rank, hated moneylenders. Yet though the Lombards shared with the Jews the bad image of moneylenders in Christendom, the hostility and even aversion they provoked did not turn into persecution, as it did for the Jews, because there was no religious or historical dimension to the poor image they presented to Christians.[5]

Alongside the moneylenders were the moneychangers, from whom they were not always distinguished. They first came to prominence, as we have seen, at the end of the twelfth century, and they performed a function that became indispensable due to the increasing diversity of currencies. They carried out their activities on a bench or table, in full view, in a shop open to the street, like all craftsmen. They clustered together so as to facilitate the transactions of their clients, who often drew on the services of more than one of them. In Bruges they kept their table close to the Grand-Place and great cloth hall, in Florence their *banchi in mercato* were in the Mercato Vecchio and the Mercato Nuovo, in Venice on the Ponte di Rialto and in Genoa close to the Casa di San Giorgio. They performed two traditional functions: moneychanging, from which they took their name, and the trade in precious metals. They were the principal suppliers of the latter to the mint, receiving these metals from their customers in the form of ingots or, more often, plate. According to circumstances, they also exported these precious metals, in spite of the theoretical monopoly of the moneyers. Through these operations they had a great influence on the prices of precious metals and their fluctuations.

Monetary mutations

The difficulties visible from the end of the thirteenth century in the monetary sphere were also revealed by changes in the value of the coins in use, known as monetary mutations. I draw here on the remarkable presentation of this phenomenon in Marc Bloch's *Esquisse d'une histoire monétaire de l'Europe*. Medieval coins generally circulated at a legal rate fixed by whichever public authority had the right to mint coins and put them into circulation: lords, bishops and, increasingly, princes and kings. Alongside this legal rate, there was also a 'commercial' or 'voluntary' rate, defined by trading circles, but secondary and fluctuating. This dual rate remained globally stable for a long time. At the end of the thirteenth century, however, the possessors of minting rights began to alter the exchange value expressed in the monetary unit, on the one hand, and in the weight of metal, on the other. These modifications are called mutations. They could be made in both directions: it was possible to 'strengthen' a currency by increasing the weight of metal corresponding to a given monetary unit; it was also possible to weaken it. The most numerous monetary mutations, and the most important, were weakenings, not strengthenings, what we today call devaluations. The value system of money was complicated in the thirteenth century by the resumption of the minting of gold and the establishment within Christendom of a system of bimetallism. The value of the coins thus depended on three different elements which conjoined, the weight in precious metal, the value in relation to other currencies and the value in relation to the money of account. From about 1270, in France, the kingdom of Naples, Venice and the Roman Curia, the price of gold rose. The king of France, here taken as reference, was forced to carry out a first mutation in 1290, but the rise in the price of precious metals continued, and Philip the Fair had to decree further mutations in 1295 and 1303. Attempts to return to what was called 'good' money, in 1306, 1311 and 1313, failed. After Philip the Fair, therefore, there was a further series of devaluations, between 1318 and 1330. The mutation of 1318–22 affected in particular the gros tournois, that of 1322–6 concerned primarily the agnel, and between 1326 and 1329 the royal government proved unable to prevent a new fall, and what was called *monnaie fondante*, or 'melting money'.[6]

The mutations were not aimed solely at adapting monetary circulation to economic realities. For the princes, and in particular for the king of France, who lacked an adequate tax system, they were also a way of gaining money by reducing their indebtedness. However, these measures were to the disadvantage of merchants and wage earners and provoked a strong hostile reaction to the royal government. The monetary mutations were one of the principal causes of the popular revolts and political troubles of the fourteenth century. That the king should assure 'good', that is, stable, money became a popular demand, encouraged by the reactions to these mutations. It was from the latter that Philip the Fair acquired the pejorative nickname 'False-moneyer'.

Yet, right up to the sixteenth century, many 'false' acts were fabricated and circulated without any problem – one need think only of the false Donation of Constantine, forged in the eighth century at Rome and justifying the existence of the pontifical states. Throughout virtually the whole of the Middle Ages, imitations of Byzantine and Muslim coins circulated freely in Christendom. The pejorative notion of 'false moneying' was linked to the birth of states claiming to be sovereign, a post-feudal notion, and to the gradual institution of a regalian right over currencies, violations of which involved what came to be called 'lese-majesty'. The fourteenth and fifteenth centuries saw several cases of exceptionally harsh repression of false moneying, which amounted to the usurpation of the regalian right to mint coins. In the thirteenth century, punishment by a form of cruel death, such as putting out the eyes or boiling in a cauldron, occasionally referred to in the kingdom of France, may have been largely theoretical.

The 'victory of gold'

The monetary stability of Europe was also disrupted by what Peter Spufford has called the 'victory of gold'. He believes that, after the return to bimetallism in the thirteenth century, gold became pre-eminent in the gold–silver pair, which changed the relative values of the two metals. Although hardly comparable to those of Africa or the East, a gold mine of some importance at Kremnica, in Hungary, was more intensively exploited after c.1320. The availability of gold, imported from Hungary, and above all from Africa and the East, the traditional regions of supply, greatly increased at the beginning of the fourteenth century. The chief centre of convergence and redistribution was Venice. Gold re-exported through Venice supplied many mints. The most important of these was probably that of Florence where, according to the chronicler Giovanni Villani, the town mint, around 1340, struck between 350,000 and 400,000 gold florins a year. In France, the minting and circulation of gold, previously largely confined to Paris, spread throughout most of the kingdom, especially when King Philip VI stepped up his expenditure in preparation for the Hundred Years War. The minting and circulation of gold also spread to the Rhône Valley, facilitating the heavy spending of the Avignon popes, in particular Clement VI, between 1342 and 1352. It was only at the end of the 1330s that large numbers of gold coins reached north-western Europe, though more, it seems, for political than for commercial reasons. Like Philip VI of France, Edward III of England used gold to buy allies in the opening stages of the Hundred Years War. His principal lenders, as we have seen, were the Florentine bankers, especially the Bardi and the Peruzzi. The most costly of his allies was the duke of Brabant, who was promised some 360,000 florins. Edward III also bought the military assistance of the Emperor Louis of Bavaria, while Philip VI paid for the support of the count of Flanders and the king of Bohemia. These payments meant that gold coins frequently replaced silver ingots in the mints of Brabant, Hainault, Guelders and Cambrai, where gold coins were struck for the first time in 1336–7. The Florentine florin and its imitations and the gold écu of France were joined in Germany by the gold coins increasingly struck by the archbishops of Cologne, Mainz and Trier, the bishop of Bamberg and a few lay lords. The mints were concentrated in the valleys of the Rhine and the Main. In the zone of the Hanseatic League, only the mint of Lübeck struck gold coins, from 1340, though it continued to strike silver coins too. The Lübeck gold coins seem not to have been linked to the political schemes that had dominated elsewhere but were intended simply to facilitate trade with Bruges.

The practice of making payments in gold soon spread to trade. In particular, the price of that great medieval export product, English wool, rose greatly from around 1340 and, with the aid of Florentine moneyers attracted to England, Edward III had minted a gold coin called the noble. England also began to have the ransoms of the most famous prisoners of the Hundred Years War paid in gold coin, as in the case of King John II the Good of France, taken captive at the Battle of Poitiers (1356). In spite of the exploitation of the gold mines of Hungary, only very small quantities of gold coins were struck in central and eastern Europe before the sixteenth century; the exception was the Hungarian ducat whose circulation increased in line with the expansion of production in the gold mines of Hungary. In Florence and Venice, gold coins were so widespread from the mid-fourteenth century that they came to replace silver coins as the most frequently used coin of account. Gold was still imported from Africa, in particular from Sidjilmassa in Morocco, which impressed the great Muslim writers and travellers of the mid-fourteenth century and facilitated the trade of Arab merchants between the Sahara and Italy and, above all, Spain. The supply of African gold made it possible for the Spanish mints to strike gold doblas in Castile and gold florins in Aragon.

Attempts at stabilization

The monetary mutations and the disturbances they created, as was to be expected in a society where the economic was part of a global political and religious system, gave rise to a highly influential work which remains one of the masterpieces of medieval scholasticism to deal with what we call the economy. This was the *De moneta*, the work of a Parisian academic, Nicole Oresme (c.1320–82), who was associated with one of the most famous colleges of the faculty of arts of the University of Paris, the College of Navarre, of which he was Grand Master from 1356 to 1361. It was here that he wrote his treatise, initially in Latin, then in French, sometime before 1360. In the fourteenth century, this work was regarded as of lesser importance within a very rich oeuvre consisting of translations of and commentaries on Aristotle and works on mathematics, music, physics, astronomy and cosmology (in which he vigorously denounced astrology and the magical and divinatory arts). Yet the *De moneta* is today the best known and most admired of the writings of Oresme. In this treatise, which is more political in nature, he shows the damaging effects of monetary mutations and the need for kings to ensure stable money; he emphasizes that money, though a regalian prerogative, was not the personal property of the king, but the common property of the people who used it. Oresme's treatise probably influenced the king of France, John II the Good, who restored the 'good money', that is, a stable currency, in the form of a gold coin, the franc. This, after the brief and unsuccessful attempt of St Louis, lasted for centuries, alongside the silver gros with fleur-de-lis, and the deniers tournois and parisis, on the 24th *pied*.[7] The decision was taken by a royal *ordonnance* promulgated at Compiègne on 5 December 1360, addressed to the mintmasters and to the bailiffs and seneschals, so as to ensure that the necessary technical and administrative work was carried out. These francs of fine gold, at the rate of 63 coins for one mark of Paris (244.75g), were destined to circulate at the rate of 20 sous tournois each.[8]

Charles V, son of John II, was deeply concerned for the stability of the currency. He made sure that a bull of 1309 of Pope Clement V excommunicating false moneyers was propagated throughout the kingdom of France and took action against counterfeiters and speculation. In 1370, he gave orders that all the coins which did not conform to the official currency rate should be devalued and could in future only be used as billon, that is, 'black money', of very low value. Monetary stability was demanded by the clergy in the interests of justice, by the merchants in the interests of the efficient conduct of their affairs and by the people as a whole for both these reasons, especially as devaluations usually led to lower wages and higher prices. Nevertheless, despite all the efforts of the European sovereigns to maintain it, debasements of the various currencies continued on and off until the sixteenth century. According to Peter Spufford, every European currency was affected between 1300 and 1500, but the debasements were greater in some countries than others. In spite of the persistence of many different currencies, the general trend for stronger nations in Christendom gave an essentially national framework to the use of money or its value of reference. In the order of loss of value, Spufford's list is as follows: England (loss of 1.5 per cent), Aragon and Venice (1.9 per cent), Bohemia (2.5 per cent), the Hanse (2.7 per cent), Florence (3 per cent), Rome (2.8 per cent), France (3.9 per cent), Austria (5 per cent), Flanders (6.1 per cent), Cologne (16.8 per cent) and Castile (65 per cent).

Monetary instability was essentially blamed on the ruler, which meant that the assemblies stepped up their efforts to limit his power. This is clear in the case of the nobility and bourgeoisie of Brabant with regard to the duke in 1314, and of the assemblies of the Langue d'Oïl in France in 1320, 1321, 1329 and 1333. The resumption of the Hundred Years War led to devaluations of the currency in France – though weak and ephemeral – in the years 1417–22 and 1427–9. Monetary mutations, as we have seen, were one of the factors which drove the urban and rural masses into rebellion, whether against the king or against the lords. As is well known, the end of the Middle Ages was an age of revolt as well as an age of war, especially in France and the Low Countries, where great merchants often played a major role in the rebellions, alongside or at the head of the people; we need only quote Etienne Marcel in Paris between 1355 and 1358, the butcher Caboche in Paris in 1413–14 and the father and son Van Artevelde in Liège in 1337 and 1381–2. It was also the case with the revolt of the textile workers, the Ciompi, in Florence, from 1375 to 1378, and in Castile in the fourteenth and fifteenth centuries, the latter being the country with both the greatest devaluations of the currency and the most numerous and most violent revolts. In 1350, a Florentine florin exchanged in Castile for 20 maravedis; in 1480, the same florin, unchanged, exchanged for around 375 maravedis. England is an example of the near-absence of monetary mutation. It owed its stability both to the continued importance of its wool exports and to the fact that, from 1352, the value of the royal English currency could be changed only by an act of Parliament.

The weaknesses of the tax systems

The care lavished by governments, particularly royal, on monetary stability, with more success in some cases than others, was not paralleled by a similar concern for the organization of taxation. One of the great roles played by money in the Middle Ages, together with its use in the growth of trade and daily exchanges, was to encourage the appearance and augmentation of the need for resources on the part of the nascent states. As we have seen, that crucial medieval phenomenon, the assumption of public power by centralized states, or states in gestation, sought and to some extent found in money the means necessary to its achievement. We have already observed the beginnings of this process. It was given a decisive impulse in the reigns of Henry II (1154–89) in England and Philip Augustus (1180–1223) in France, and in the pontifical states under Innocent III (1198–1216) and then under the Avignon popes (1309–78).

In the classic feudal regime, as we have seen, the king, as principal lord, was originally expected to 'live off his own', that is, to live off the revenues from the royal demesne. Although demesnes were enlarged in the thirteenth and fourteenth centuries, particularly in France, they became increasingly inadequate as a way of financing the great lordships, and above all the monarchic states, which employed an increasing number of servants at every level. Similarly, the role of the great lords and sovereigns was strengthened in the administrative, judicial and economic spheres, in particular by the minting of coins, while the growing splendour of seigneurial and royal pomp in clothing, festivities, gifts and so on made it necessary for them to procure from their subjects exceptional resources of the sort that we today lump together under the general heading of taxation. A similar need for exceptional resources was experienced by the towns, which generally became independent from the twelfth century, and also increasingly dependent on local resources. The first justification for an exceptional tax of this sort was provided by the crusades. The king of France, for example, levied an exceptional tax called the tithe, which was continued after the crusades. It was intended to maintain order in the kingdom and, from the end of the thirteenth century and especially during the period of the Avignon popes, it was shared with the papacy.

As is well known, the fourteenth and to a lesser extent fifteenth centuries were marked by a demographic collapse which had probably begun earlier in the fourteenth century, which had seen a major famine in 1317–18, and when population decline produced what have been called 'deserted villages'. This demographic crisis was made much worse after 1348 by the series of epidemics of the Black Death, that is, bubonic plague. War was also, as I have said, a heavy drain on the financial resources of towns, princes and states.

Apart from the more or less serious problem of demography, the tax systems of the last two centuries of the traditional Middle Ages suffered both ups and downs: states needed to lay their hands on larger revenues linked to the growth of their powers but the resistance of their populations usually made it impossible for them to establish a stable fiscal system before the sixteenth century. The state which seemed to be most successful in developing its fiscal practice, that of the Church, also had its successes and its failures. The standardizing action of the Apostolic Camera and the use of lay bankers made the Avignon papacy the greatest financial power in Christendom in the first half of the fourteenth century. Relations were generally friendly with the Italian towns and states and, for a while, with the kingdom of France; however, the Holy Roman Empire strongly resisted pontifical claims in Germany and there was virtually a state of perpetual war between the English monarchy and the Holy See over taxation. The situation was in some ways similar in fifteenth-century France. Of the two principal fiscal revenues of the papacy, the tithes, which could be discounted, could be adapted to variations in the income from benefices. On the other hand, the annates, which crippled the finances of bishoprics in periods of vacancy, were not so flexible and were often very heavy. The pontifical treasury was often obliged to accept staggered payment or even allow reductions in this tax. Lastly, the Avignon papacy often had to contend with the opposition of states which saw these levies as encroachments on their financial powers.

As regards the tax problems of states and their evolution in the fourteenth and fifteenth centuries, the French example is instructive. The first tentative steps were taken under Philip the Fair (1285–1314). He and his counsellors first tried to establish more or less lasting, if not regular, taxes on market transactions. In 1291, a sales tax of a 'penny in the pound' was instituted 'for the realm', which was to apply to everyone and to last for six years. The yield from this tax was low, so in 1295 the king transferred it from sales to stocks of merchandise. This *maltôte* was a failure. Philip the Fair also sought to introduce at the national level taxes that had already been tried with some success in certain towns. These were levied on the wealth or income of every subject of the realm. They were presented as a substitute for military service, which had recently been imposed on all the male inhabitants of the kingdom, a fiction that was emphasized by the fact that the monarch declared that it applied even to the *arrière-ban*. The new taxes were levied in 1302, 1303 and 1304, and the king asked in the assemblies for the consent of the great ecclesiastics and laity and sometimes of the towns with special links to the monarchy known as the *bonnes villes*. The gabelle, introduced in 1341, had to be abolished in 1356. These efforts to impose a royal tax system were among the principal causes of the sporadic revolts of the fourteenth and early fifteenth centuries. Above all, they gave more power, on a lasting basis, to the meetings of the estates, a sort of early parliament, to which the king had to submit the introduction of new taxes. The French monarchy was also unable – perhaps did not even seek – to improve the administration of this tax system. There was no budget for the finances of the French monarchy in the fourteenth and fifteenth centuries and, thanks to the scarcity of documents providing prices or numerical data for the Middle Ages, it is very difficult to establish one. In any case, except in the build-up to large-scale military operations such as those of the Hundred Years War, the monarchy did not produce financial estimates, an exercise that was limited to a few centres of particular importance in the economic and financial sphere. As Ugo Tucci has shown, they included Venice.[9]

10

The Perfecting of the Financial System at the End of the Middle Ages

The growth of trade in the fourteenth and fifteenth centuries, though probably less vigorous than during the long thirteenth century, led to the creation of new financial instruments which made it possible to meet the growing demand for money in Christendom without resorting to a massive new provision of coin, the inadequacy of Europe's own precious metal mines and the uncertainties of the supply of precious metals from Africa and the East limiting the monetary possibilities of Europe.

Bills of exchange and insurance contracts

The two principal innovations which made it possible to meet the new needs, at least in part, in the absence of sufficient real money, were the bill of exchange and the practice of insurance. The invention of the bill of exchange was a consequence not only of the unsatisfied need for coin already referred to but also of the reactions of medieval merchants to the seasonal variations in the money market. These variations were caused by a number of factors: the dates at which fairs were held, the quality of the harvests and their distribution throughout the year; the arrivals and departures of maritime commercial convoys; and the financial and accounting practices of governments. As we have seen, the introduction of money into feudal rent had modified the traditional calendar: Michaelmas (at the end of September) and All Saints (at the beginning of November) became major payment dates. The need for money might fluctuate for other reasons. One Venetian merchant noted in the mid-fifteenth century:

> In Genoa, money is dear in September, January and April, due to the departure of the boats...in Rome, where the pope resides, the price of money varies according to the number of vacant benefices and the movements of the pope, who increases the price of money wherever he goes...in Valence it is dear in July and August because of the corn and the rice...in Montpellier, there are three fairs which are the cause of a great dearness of money there...

The principle of the bill of exchange was defined by the Belgian historian Raymond De Roover as follows:

> an agreement by which a deliverer, usually a merchant-banker, gave a certain sum of money in local currency to another merchant [the 'taker'] and received from him a letter missive which was payable at a future date (credit transaction), in another place, and in another currency (exchange transaction). By definition such a contract involved *both* a credit and an exchange transaction.

Here is a bill of exchange taken from the archive of Francesco di Marco Datini of Prato:

> In the name of God, 18th December 1399, pay by this first letter at usance to Brunacio di Guido and Co. CCCCLXXII livres X sous of Barcelona, which 472 livres 10 sous worth 900 écus at 10 sous 6 deniers per écu have been paid to me here by Riccardo degl'Alberti and Co. Pay them in good and true form and charge them to my account. May God preserve you.
>
> Ghuiglielmo Barberi
> Greetings from Bruges
> [in another hand] Accepted 12 January 1399 [1400].
> [On the back] Francesco di Marco and Co., at Barcelona
> First [letter].

This is a bill paid in Barcelona by the 'drawee' or payer (the Barcelona branch of the Datini firm) to the 'beneficiary' or payee (the firm of Brunacio di Guido, also in Barcelona) at the request of the 'taker' or drawer (Ghuiglielmo Barberi, Italian merchant of Bruges) to whom the 'deliverer' or remitter (the house of Riccardo degl'Alberti in Bruges) had paid 900 écus at 10 sous 6 deniers per écu.

Ghuiglielmo Barberi, an exporter of Flemish cloth in regular contact with Catalonia, had arranged for money to be advanced in Flemish écus by the Bruges branch of the Alberti, the great Florentine merchant bankers. Anticipating the sale of the merchandise that he had dispatched to his correspondent in Barcelona, the house of Datini, he drew on them a draft to be paid in Barcelona to the local correspondent of the Alberti, the house of Brunacio di Guido and Co. This was both a credit and an exchange transaction. The payment was made in Barcelona on 11 February 1400, thirty days after its acceptance on 12 January. This delay was the 'usance', which varied according to the places involved (it was customarily thirty days between Bruges and Barcelona). This made it possible to verify the authenticity of the bill of exchange and, as necessary, procure the money.

Thus the bill of exchange met four potential needs on the part of a merchant and offered him four possibilities:

(a) a means of payment for a commercial transaction
(b) a way of transferring funds – between places using different currencies
(c) a source of credit
(d) a financial gain by exploiting the differences and variations in the exchange rate in the various places in the conditions I described above.

In fact, over and above the commercial transactions, there could be a trade in bills of exchange between two or, more often, three places. This market was very active in the fourteenth and fifteenth centuries, and the occasion for speculation on a large scale.[1]

On the other hand, medieval merchants seem not to have been familiar with the practices of endorsement or discounting, which date only from the sixteenth century. A very basic technique, that of the debenture, a simple order of payment, was found at the end of the Middle Ages in the sphere of the Hanse.

Medieval historians have recently debated the notion of risk. I have already referred to the work of Alain Guerreau and noted my disagreement with his negative ideas on this point, even if what we call money was less clearly linked in the minds of medieval people to the modern notions of risk, peril or danger than it is today. Anticipation, which follows from an awareness of risk, seems by the thirteenth century to have concerned business circles in certain parts of Christendom where financial commitments could be on a large scale, in particular Venice. In any case, both thinking and practice in this sphere, especially in case of peril at sea, that byword for danger for medieval people, led to the appearance in the thirteenth century of contracts with the name of *securitas* (security); these were forerunners of contracts that became more common in the fourteenth and fifteenth centuries and constituted true contracts of insurance. I take the liberty here of citing a text I have already used in my earlier study.[2] In a register on whose title page are written the words: 'This is a register of Francesco di Prato and Co., residing in Pisa, in which I will write all the insurances I make for others; may God make this profitable for me and protect me from dangers', we read, for 3 August 1384:

> We insure Baldo Ridolfi and Co. for 100 gold florins of wool, loaded onto the boat of Bartolomeo Vitale in transit from Penisola to Porto Pisano. Of these 100 florins which we insure against all risk, we will receive four gold florins in cash as testified by an act by the hand of Gherardo d'Ormaumo which we have countersigned.

Below is a note to the effect that 'the said boat arrived safely 4 August 1384 and we are discharged of the said risks.' Nevertheless, this notion of risk, and the associated notion of anticipation did not give rise to specific, official acts until after the Middle Ages, with the slow growth of capitalism.

From lender to banker

The use of money led above all to a rapid expansion of accounting, both in its methods and in the amount of paperwork it generated. The great merchants and commercial companies kept numerous specialized account books and, in particular, a 'secret book'. In this, as already noted, they kept a record of the text of the partnership, the amount of each partner's contribution to the capital, the figures from which it was possible to calculate each partner's position in the society at any given moment and the distribution of profits and losses. Nevertheless, we should not see this accounting, which reached a remarkable level of competence and flexibility, as evidence of a society in which money played a major role. On the contrary, the techniques of money remained strictly limited in the Middle Ages, both as regards the social sphere in which they were used and the level of the scientific knowledge that resulted. It is true that the great medieval merchants developed a remarkable technique for keeping their accounts, that is, the double-entry bookkeeping already referred to. In reality, however, they were no more than tiny isolated islands in a vast medieval sea, the majority of people remaining remote from sophisticated practices in the case of everything we would put under the heading of money.[3] At most we may accept that money, however limited its role in the Middle Ages, acted as a stimulus in the spheres of writing and commercial bookkeeping and in arithmetic applied to the necessities of daily life.

This is one reason why it is difficult to identify within this business world a category of professionals consisting of bankers in the strict sense of the word. The boundaries between the various specialists in the use of money, that is, the Lombards, who were mainly lenders, the moneychangers and the bankers strictly speaking, were by no means always clear. Lending remained the speciality of the Lombards, at least in the thirteenth and fourteenth centuries. The documentation for their loans is sadly incomplete but it has been possible to compile lists for certain towns and periods. The edition by Giulia Scarcia of Register 9-1 in the Public Archives of Freiburg, in Germany, has shown that, in the years 1355–8, the customers of the Lombard moneylenders came primarily from the upper ranks of the middle classes, including knights and nobles as well as burgesses.[4] The practice of lending was on such a large scale in fourteenth- and fifteenth-century Italy that it has been convincingly argued that a series of bills of exchange issued in Milan in 1445–50 were in reality loans.[5] Just as the Lombards occupied a lower economic and social level than the great bankers of the period, so most of those who handled money in the fourteenth and fifteenth centuries were merchants and engaged in all the transactions in which monetary value was at issue. A hierarchy existed between them, to the point where, in Florence or Bruges, for example, people spoke of *banchi grossi*. One in every thirty-five or forty people in fifteenth-century Bruges had an account with one of these Lombards, but 80 per cent of the Lombards' customers had a balance of account below 50 Flemish livres.

The true bankers, inasmuch as they existed, were often traders for whom precious metals and coins became commodities. This may have begun with the conclusion of contracts of partnership for a specific commercial operation, which were sometimes not only renewed but also turned into a lasting association. As we have seen, the Venetians played a special role in defining two types of association, the *compagnia* and the *societas terrae*.

In the *compagnia*, the contracting parties were bound closely together and shared risks and hopes, profits and losses. The *societas terrae* was closer to the *commenda*. The lender alone bore the risks of loss while the profits were generally shared equally. However, there was great flexibility in many of their clauses: the proportions of capital invested might vary greatly and the length of the association was usually not limited to a single operation or single voyage but fixed for a given period of time – usually of between one and four years. Lastly, many intermediate types, combining various aspects of both, existed between these basic forms of the *compagnia* and the *societas*. The complexity of these contracts found expression in documents of such length that is impracticable to quote examples here.

Complex and powerful organisms grew up around certain merchants, certain families and certain groups which have traditionally been given the name of 'companies' in the modern sense of the word.[6] The most famous and the best known were directed by illustrious Florentine families, some of which I have already mentioned, such as the Peruzzi, the Bardi and the Medici. It should be noted, however, that, according to their historians, chief among them Armando Sapori, it is possible to detect major differences between the structure of these companies in the thirteenth and fourteenth centuries and in the fifteenth century, at least in the case of Italy.

These societies continued to be based on contracts which bound the parties for only a single commercial operation or limited period of time. However, the practice of regularly renewing some of these contracts, the presence throughout a vast economic area of the same names, who provided substantial capital for large-scale and regularly repeated enterprises, and all these commercial ties formed around a few individuals turned the latter into the heads of stable organizations transcending the ephemeral character of the specific operations and contracts which defined them. In the thirteenth and fourteenth centuries, these veritable commercial houses remained highly centralized. They were headed by one or more merchants who had a network of branches and were represented, away from the main base where the director or directors resided, by salaried employees. In the fifteenth century, a house such as that of the Medici was decentralized. It consisted of a combination of separate associations, each with its own capital and each with its own geographical base. Thus the mother house of Florence had subsidiaries in London, Bruges, Geneva, Lyon, Avignon, Milan, Venice and Rome, which were managed by directors who were only in part and secondarily salaried employees, and who were primarily backers, owners of a part of the capital – like Angelo Tani, Tommaso Portinari, Simone Neri, Amerigo Benci and so on. The Medici of Florence were the link which held all these houses together only because they were usually the largest providers of capital in each and because they centralized the accounts, information and direction of affairs. It only needed a Lorenzo, less attentive than his grandfather Cosimo, to let things slide, and the branches began to go their own way. Conflicts developed within the firm and cracks appeared in the edifice; the result was ruin, made all the easier by the large number of people now involved, as participation seems to have become deposit. Once the deposits of money represented a large part of the firm's capital and reserves, it was made more vulnerable by the needs, hesitations, demands and fears of these depositors, who had fewer scruples in reclaiming their money than the old partners, bound together by ties of family and commercial collaboration.

The career of Jacques Coeur

In exceptional cases, certain money men rose to an elevated position in the social and political hierarchy. I will quote a famous example, all the more interesting in that the man in question was not Italian, like most members of this social category, but French.

I refer, of course, to Jacques Coeur, who came from Bourges. Michel Mollat, who devoted a fine book to Jacques Coeur,[7] was quite rightly struck by the diversity of his activities and of the places in which he operated. Indeed, he claimed that 'a map that reproduced the distribution of these interests would correspond to an economic map of France in the middle of the fifteenth century.' In fact, this claim is only valid if this is defined as the geographical diversity of the active presence of Jacques Coeur. It is not a true economic map of France, because, even under the impact of royal policy, such an economy did not exist in the whole of the country; rather, it was a collection of unstructured places and activities. Jacques Coeur acquired property here and there, landed estates, assignments of landed rents – it has been claimed that the fifteenth century was the great century of landed rent, which shows the continued economic and social importance of land ownership – and costly *hôtels* in Bourges, Saint-Pourçain, Tours, Lyon and Montpellier, which were assertions of prestige, not business premises. He amassed remunerative activities which, thanks to the evolution of Christian doctrine, managed to escape condemnation as usury, for example taking advantage of the inchoate and disorderly development of the tax system, farms, aids and *gabelles*. Having grasped the importance of war as a source of expenditure and profit, he supplied harness and weapons to the royal troops and did well out of ransoming English prisoners. He also directed the royal Argenterie, wardrobes and *entrepôts*, sign that his activities had not broken all links with thesauration. He had interests in Florence, in Spain and in Bruges. Outside France and its neighbours, his principal sphere of activity was the Mediterranean. Indeed, after falling into disgrace, being imprisoned and escaping, he ended his life on the island of Chios, in the Aegean, where he died in 1456. His principal office had been that of Master of the King's Mints from 1436 until his escape from prison.

11

Towns, States and Money at the End of the Middle Ages

Urban debts and taxes

By the end of the Middle Ages, the towns had usually increased the extent of their resources, not through the growth of trade, which had been badly hit by wars and not yet recovered the vigour it would achieve in the sixteenth century, but because they had expanded their suburbs and the territory over which they had established control and from which they drew wealth, men and power. For proof, one need only quote the famous frescoes of Ambrogio Lorenzetti in Siena ('The Effects of Good and Bad Government'), which date from the mid-fourteenth century. The towns had put the organization of their financial institutions on a sounder footing, especially the Courts of Accounts. They were badly affected, nevertheless, by one of the great curses of fifteenth-century society, indebtedness. This was both collective, that is, the public debt, and individual, and it mainly took the form of the sale of annuities. Historians have observed a spiralling of debt from the mid-fifteenth century in the Low Countries, in the case of Brussels, Lille, Leiden, Malines and Namur. The same situation was found in the German towns, for example, Hamburg and Basel, where indebtedness, which had been around 1 per cent in 1362, exceeded 50 per cent by the mid-fifteenth century. It was also the case in the Iberian Peninsula: in Barcelona, the debt absorbed 42 per cent of revenue in 1358 and 61 per cent in 1403;

in Valence, indebtedness rose from 37.5 per cent in 1365 to 76 per cent in 1485. Nor were the great Italian financial centres immune from this phenomenon.

This indebtedness not only aggravated the antagonisms between the various social categories but also led to a certain loss of confidence in the urban system and disaffection with urban patriotism. As the towns were simultaneously suffering encroachments on their power at the hands of princes and kings, the indebtedness helped to weaken urban power and the urban image at a number of levels. Europe had become in large part, in the thirteenth century, a Europe of towns. It was largely financial problems that were responsible for the gradual subjection of these towns to the princes. The Middle Ages of the towns was not a Middle Ages of money. The princes, who had access to coercive powers for procuring money not available to the towns, were able to remain at the head of their states when, at a later stage, money assumed a dominant role. As has been observed of the Late Middle Ages, 'the debt generated an unstoppable spiral which fed on itself by provoking a dizzy escalation in municipal spending... the towns found it increasingly difficult to make payments within the specified period and arrears accumulated.'[1] The only people to benefit were the lenders, who were unquestionably rich men.

Three studies, of Dijon, Frankfurt-am-Main and the towns of the ephemeral Burgundian state, reveal the seriousness of the problems affecting urban finances at the end of the Middle Ages. The Chambre des comtes in Dijon was reorganized in 1386 and its archives have been analysed by F. Humbert and Henri Dubois.[2] Like that of most towns, the tax system in Dijon was based on a range of levies.

1 The *fouages* (hearth taxes) granted to the dukes by the Estates of the duchy were irregular both in timing and in yield. In 1386, for example, the income from these *fouages* rose to 3,219 francs 8 gros.
2 The town levied a tax to finance the upkeep of the ramparts.

Other taxes, by contrast, were levied regularly: the *gabelle*, or salt tax (for which the records have not survived) and the tax called *des marcs*, consisting of one hundredth of the *vaillant*[3] of each taxpayer, levied annually for the benefit of the duke.

Lastly, two proportional taxes were based on the sale of goods, the twentieth paid on all transactions and the eighth levied on retail sales of wine.

These various taxes were farmed out to citizens under the control of the receiver of the *bailliage* of Dijon. In 1386–7, there were thirty-five farms, and they provide the historian with information about the economic activity of the town and its territory. Easily the most profitable was the farm of wine, which accounted for 22 per cent of the total. Next came cloth, corn and legumes, meat, leathers, cattle and pigs, bread and flour, each of which brought in around 200 francs. The preponderance of foodstuffs is clear. The sum of these farms, and thus of the activity whose scale they reveal, remained fairly stable until the beginning of the fourteenth century. In the principal urban centres elsewhere in the duchy, the farm of wool fell markedly. The farmers of the twentieth were usually men of some standing who practised a craft and whose activities were rarely confined to financial operations. Dubois has emphasized that they formed neither a group nor a homogenous milieu. They included, on the one hand, high servants of the prince and, on the other, members of the social elite, one might even say patriciate, who added the profit from these farms to other forms of income and sources of prestige. It is impossible, therefore, to identify in the Dijon of c.1400 persons who can be defined primarily as 'money men'. Money was only one of the factors bestowing prestige in urban circles.

Pierre Monnet has studied for Frankfurt-am-Main in the fourteenth century what he has called 'the financing of urban independence by the moneyed elites'.[4] He focuses on two events which involved the amassing of large sums of money. The first was the purchase in 1372 by the council of the imperial city of Frankfurt of the last rights of the king-emperor who was its lord. The council spent between 25,000 and 26,000 florins to assure a firm basis for its independence. An imperial agent, the *Reichsschultheiss*, responsible for all the royal revenues in its territory (rents, mills, pools, demesnes, etc.), had played an essential role in the town. In 1389, the town introduced a tax on the output of the principal crafts, the grocers, tailors, bakers and shoemakers. In 1407, the clergy were made subject to the majority of urban taxes, in particular that on wine. The total tax burden doubled between 1379 and 1389. The second crucial event came in 1389 when the town suffered a catastrophe when its army was beaten by a coalition of nobles; 620 prisoners were taken and a ransom of 73,000 florins had to be paid. However, the town was able to cope with this by drafting onto the council members of the old patriciate whose experience and multifarious sources of income made it possible to avoid the indebtedness afflicting many other towns, and which was, as I have already observed, the great evil of the Late Middle Ages in the financial sphere. Frankfurt was even able to assist the town of Wetzlar, which had accumulated a debt of 80,000 florins, with a gift of 24,000 florins. The phenomenon was probably at its worst in Mainz, which was never able to emerge from a debt which had reached 375,000 livres by 1447. I quote, to conclude this brief survey of the finances of Frankfurt-am-Main, the perceptive observation of Pierre Monnet: 'the prosperity of the town was not achieved to the benefit of new men or new rich men, but rather in favour of an elite of a different type, who were already in possession of both power and wealth.'

A final glimpse of urban finances and the urban tax system is provided by Marc Boone's study of the Flemish towns of the ephemeral late medieval Burgundian state.[5] Flanders had an exceptionally high urban density in the fourteenth and fifteenth centuries. If we omit the French part of the county, the rest was dominated by three large towns: Ghent, with around 64,000 inhabitants, Bruges, with around 45,000, and Ypres, around 28,000. However, there were also fifty small and medium-sized towns with fewer than 10,000 inhabitants, and the population density for the county as a whole was as high as 77.9 inhabitants per square kilometre. These towns were characteristically both great centres of production – for textiles, luxury goods and more everyday items – and major exchange markets, supplied by colonies of foreign merchants. A single centre played a prime role in the distribution and redistribution of products, which was Bruges until the mid-fifteenth century and then Antwerp. Far from being impoverished by comital rule, the latter, by making itself the principal lender to the counts, found it a major route to great wealth. The tax system was gradually taken over by farmers belonging to the patriciate, who excluded the professionals in credit, pawnbrokers, usurers, Lombards and moneychangers of every type. The latter were ruled out as lenders to the town, too. This patriciate was also often responsible for the administration of the county on behalf of the prince. In 1410, for example, the principal tax, the assize on wine, was taken at farm by an association consisting of the members of the Utenhove family, an old patrician family of Ghent, many of whom had been receivers or bailiffs of the count, and Master Simon de Fourmelles, a lawyer-notary who had served Dukes John the Fearless and Philip the Good, and then been president of the Council of Flanders, the highest court of justice in the county.

State finances and tax systems: the Holy See

The states, consolidating their administrations during the fourteenth and fifteenth centuries, found they needed more money and tried to improve the organization of their finances and tax systems; the income drawn directly from the landed estates of the prince was overtaken by taxation as the main source of finance for the activities of central governments. As in the case of the long thirteenth century, I will take as examples the pontifical states, well known to have been pioneers in this sphere, and France.

We are particularly well informed about pontifical finances as they have been the subject of excellent major studies by Bernard Guillemain and Jean Favier.[6] By settling in Avignon, the pope oddly located himself at the level of a prince of a particular power more than the leader of the Church, which he had been in Rome and Italy until forced by the social situation to leave. By the time of the first of the Avignon popes, Clement V (1305–14), the princely activities of the popes led to an increase in the expenditure of the pontifical state. The pontifical court rapidly came to consist of some four or five hundred people of every rank, a hundred more than in Rome at the time of the last Roman pope, Boniface VIII. Clement V, as Guillemain has shown in his study of the accounts for the fourth year of his papacy, which is particularly well documented, spent 120,000 florins, 30,000 of them on his household: wages, food, wax, wood, fodder, laundry, the upkeep of horses and almsgiving. The non-domestic expenses were the purchase of parchment and – already – paper and the wages of chaplains, notaries and messengers. The income came first from the overlordship exercised by the Holy See: the rents owed by the king of Naples and other Italian lords and the St Peter's Pence paid by the Scandinavian kingdoms. However, these revenues were not always paid in full by those who owed them, in spite of frequent excommunications. The sums which new bishops and abbots were required to pay on election or appointment brought in 26,000 florins. Some arrears of tenths, notes Favier, completed the revenues. Clement V spent a large part of the pontifical income on gifts to great persons whose favour and protection he wished to attract, such as the kings of France and England, but mostly to his family – he was a notable nepotist. The Church, since at least the pontificate of Innocent III (1198–1216), had organized its financial levies on Christian society, as we have seen. However, the pontifical court had not yet reached this point. An essential threshold was crossed by Jean XXII (1316–34), who extended pontifical taxes to every benefice.

Two developments added greatly to the needs of the pontifical court: the construction of the Palace of the Popes in Avignon, between 1345 and 1360, and the spread of wars waged in Italy against enemies of the pontifical states. What we find here are two major activities which both accelerated and increased the use of money in the Middle Ages: building and war. The pontifical state in Avignon was thus driven to step up its exactions from the time of the pontificate of Clement VI (1342–52). The main source of income was the increased control over benefices, which took two forms: the direct appointment by the pope of incumbents of benefices in return for a share of the revenues assigned to them, and the confiscation by the Holy See of the income from vacant benefices. The pontifical finances were unexpectedly greatly enriched as a consequence of the great catastrophe which struck Christian Europe in 1348, the Black Death. The death of incumbents of benefices due to the epidemic meant a rapid increase in pontifical resources as a consequence of the reservation of benefices. Pontifical greed aggravated the conflicts between the Holy See, the national Churches and the princes. This was the case in particular with Germany and England, where the conflicts were of long standing. It has been argued that the fiscal greed of the Avignon papacy was one of the distant causes of the Reformation. The power of the Holy See over the benefices produced a new source of income. The clergy acquired the habit, often very prematurely, of addressing petitions to the pope with a view to obtaining a benefice even when it was still occupied by its incumbent. These petitions, to increase their chances of success, were frequently accompanied by gifts to the Holy See. As early as 1309, according to Favier, a cleric from Aragon bringing a petition to Avignon wrote: 'nobody believes you can do anything by entitlement or pity or charity if you don't have any money.'

The fiscal demands of the Avignon papacy were sometimes so heavy that the clergy who were its victims were unable to pay and procured reductions in the sums demanded. Another consequence of these excesses was that payment of the annates levied on the main benefices and 'common services', instead of being made in one go, as had traditionally been the case, was spread out over several instalments. The Avignon papacy also developed an old but previously limited practice, that of bargaining with lay princes for a grant to the latter of the income from a particular tax demanded by the Church. This practice, though not entirely new, had become fairly general at the time of the crusades, which it had been intended partly to finance. The Christian princes resumed the practice in the fourteenth century, which encouraged the Church to keep referring to the possibility of a new crusade. We encounter once again the link between money and war, all the more remarkable in that the war in question had religious motives and was in any case by now illusory, as history would show. Yet another procedure for procuring money dreamed up by the Avignon papacy was procurations; ecclesiastics of high rank, bishops, archdeacons and deans, were obliged to make regular visits to the churches under their jurisdiction, for which they received travel expenses. Pope Innocent IV abolished these 'procurations' in the thirteenth century, making it obligatory for free hospitality to be provided for visiting prelates. The Avignon popes not only restored procurations but also reserved half of them to the Holy See. Like most of the increases or innovations of the papacy in fiscal matters, this practice, described by Jean Favier as a true misappropriation, was justified by the Holy See on the grounds of the expenses it faced in connection with the battle against heresy; yet heresy, as is well known, was less virulent in the fourteenth than in the thirteenth century. We see how money motivated the papacy to maintain a misleading image of religious reality and of the role of the 'Roman' Church. Crusades and heresies persisted in the Christian imagination in order to satisfy the financial appetites of the Church.

In spite of the cost of its palace and its military operations in Italy, the Avignon papacy was generally regarded in the fourteenth century as a particularly wealthy community. Apart from the popes, its most eminent members, the cardinals and prelates, grew rich in these conditions. Also, in a society where indebtedness was on the increase, they played a far from negligible role as lenders. However, ecclesiastical tradition meant that they were more likely than the other lenders in Christian Europe to deal in precious objects as well as monetary values and they generally accepted items of silver or gold as security for their loans. Of the many examples of such securities given by Jean Favier, I quote here that of Cardinal Guillaume d'Aigrefeuille, who, in 1373, received as security two gold crosses adorned with emeralds, pearls, sapphires and cameos, silver plate, candelabra and even the silver throne which had belonged to Clement VI, that is, 30 gold marks and 1,600 silver marks.

One of the main problems faced by the papacy was the transfer to Avignon of the sums collected all over Christendom. The transport of goods by road was threatened by the insecurity which plagued much of Europe, especially in the fourteenth century, when looting by the mercenaries known as *routiers* was widespread. It seemed a better bet to make use of the banks, especially as the establishment of the papacy in Avignon had tempted many bankers to that town. However, two other circumstances worked in the opposite direction. On the one hand, Christendom was not yet familiar with banking practices, and the network of banks capable of assuring exchange transactions on a regular basis was very limited. Outside Italy, such banks existed almost only in London, Bruges, Paris, Montpellier, Barcelona and Lisbon. On the other hand, the banks were afraid of being led into failure by taking on too many loans, as had happened in the years 1342–6. Financial transactions worked well only with Italy, and in particular the financing by the Avignon papacy of its Italian enterprises.

All in all, the Avignon papacy enjoyed an uneven but overall very substantial increase in its income from taxation: 228,000 florins a year under Jean XXII (1316–34), 166,000 under Benedict XII (1334–42), 188,500 under Clement VI (1342–52), 253,600 with Innocent VI (1352–62), 260,000 with Urban V (1362–70) and, lastly, a great leap forward with Gregory XI (1370–8), 481,000 florins.

State finances and tax systems: the French monarchy

My second example is the French monarchy. The attempts of the kings of France in the fourteenth and fifteenth centuries to establish permanent taxes were part of a policy of rationalizing power that was never fully achieved. The institutions established by the kings had some success in controlling irregular or exceptional taxes. The Treasury, transferred to the Louvre in 1317, was managed by four treasurers, assisted by two clerks of the Treasury. During 1443–5, each of these treasurers was responsible for one area: Langue d'Oïl, Langue d'Oc, Outre-Seine and Normandy, then Guyenne, Burgundy, Picardy and Artois. They were itinerant and accountable to the Chambre des comtes, which had finally been organized, as we have seen, in 1320. This was complemented by a Cour des aides, which dealt with the problems posed by the assessment and collection of taxes, while a Cour du Trésor retained jurisdiction over the management of the royal demesne. Philip the Fair created a body that was quite separate from the Treasury, the Argenterie, a department for the provision and storage of furnishings, clothing and ornaments for the royal household. The Argenterie also financed ceremonies and festivals. Jean Favier has emphasized that its custodian, the *argentier*, was more often a merchant than a royal official, the most famous being Jacques Coeur – further proof that money had a different meaning in the Middle Ages than it has today. The Cour du Trésor fell into a fairly steady decline because of the difficulty of controlling all the financial operations of the monarchy throughout the whole of its territory; in the fifteenth century, its functions of financial control were successively absorbed by the *parlements* and the courts that were gradually created throughout the country. As for the Chambre des monnaies, the large number of mints which continued in existence deprived it of much of its theoretical power.

To be effective, taxation had to achieve a regularity which was never fully realized, primarily due to the weakness of estimates in the financial sphere and to the sustained inability of the monarchy to draw up a true national budget. The crucial period for the establishment of taxation was between 1355 and c.1370, when Kings Jean II the Good and Charles V had to find the means, first to pursue the war against the English, which had flared up again, and then to maintain the peace established by the treaty of Brétigny in 1360. As had become customary, two assemblies were consulted, one for the *pays d'oïl* and the other for the *pays d'oc*. This resulted in a redrawing of the map of the financial organization of the kingdom, which was based on the most stable administrative unit, the diocese. The established taxes were a *maltôte* on the sale of goods and a *gabelle* on salt, both fiercely contested. Around 1370, the fiscal system of the French monarchy, benefiting from experience, was established on the basis of the traditional indirect taxes, the *aides*, and a general direct tax called the *fouage*, because levied on each household, or *feu*.

Regular taxation remained immensely unpopular with the vast mass of the population. As a consequence of which, Charles V, on his deathbed, in September 1380, wishing to leave his subjects a favourable image of himself, abolished all the *fouages*, that is, direct taxes. The majority of the French population – who the king addressed as 'my people' – were only satisfied when they had obtained from his successor, or rather from the uncles who ruled in the name of the young Charles VI, the abrogation of the indirect taxes, the *aides*, as well. The fiscal problem remained acute throughout the reign of Charles VI. It aggravated the unrest of that period which culminated in the Parisian revolution of 1413 – called *cabochienne* after its popular leader, the butcher Caboche – and in the people's readiness to accept the rule of the duke of Burgundy and the Treaty of Troyes which, on the death of Charles VI, made the English child-king Henry VI ruler of France. In his struggle against the English, the dauphin, later King Charles VII, was only able to obtain from the councils he summoned temporary contributions justified by the war against the English. However, once he had established his rule over the kingdom of France, he reasserted the royal monopoly of taxation and put this into practice by means of a series of royal *ordonnances*, and then finally the Pragmatic Sanction of 1438. This reorganization led to the creation of new institutions and the sixteenth-century monarchs maintained this control over the kingdom's finances, in particular by the introduction in 1577 of financial offices, or *généralités*, which became 'the true financial and then administrative and political divisions of the kingdom of France until the Revolution.'[7]

Thus, money played an important but chaotic role in the formation of what would later be called, in France and in the rest of Europe, absolute monarchy. However, the financial basis of this regime remained fluid and uncertain, and liable to be challenged. In this sphere too, money only acquired its modern meaning in the eighteenth century.

12

Prices, Wages and Coin in the Fourteenth and Fifteenth Centuries

The last two centuries of the Middle Ages present marked contrasts in a number of ways, which have been discussed by Jérôme Baschet in a recent book.[1] For some historians it was a period of decline – 'a sad autumn', according to Johan Huizinga, author of *Herfsttij der Middeleeuwen* (*The Autumn of the Middle Ages*) – whereas for Baschet it was one of a 'continued dynamic'. There was no shortage, it is very clear, of calamities. After the Great Famine of 1315–17 came the Black Death, which erupted in 1348, killed at least a third of the Christian population and then periodically reappeared. War, whether it took the form of fierce battles, skirmishes or looting, was almost ubiquitous in the West until the middle of the fifteenth century, epitomized by the Hundred Years War between England and France. The Church split at the top and the Great Schism took the papacy to Avignon, artificial capital of Christendom, then set two, and sometimes even three, popes against each other. Taxation was essential to the functioning of a royal or communal regime, but it was difficult to impose and the princes were forced to resort to borrowing, which doomed Christendom to a state of almost perpetual crisis. Edward III of England borrowed from the Bardi of Florence, which eventually drove them into bankruptcy. Charles VII, in order to rebuild France after the Hundred Years War, borrowed from Jacques Coeur, then had to imprison him so as to avoid repaying him. The emperor Maximilian borrowed from the great Nuremberg family of Fugger, who managed to profit from his assistance, and also from the exploitation of new copper and silver mines in the Tyrol and even in Spain. However, once the Fugger had become the bankers of Charles V, on whose behalf they had paid the great electors of the Empire, and of Philip II of Spain, the bankruptcies of the Spanish monarchy ruined them and led to their disappearance in the sixteenth century. These calamities were inevitably damaging to the economy. Once peace had been restored in the mid-fifteenth century, Europe began to grow again but, as Baschet correctly observed, without everywhere achieving the high level of prosperity of the end of the long thirteenth century.

Price movements

The movement of prices and wages reflected these contrasting developments. In spite of the scarcity of numerical data, we still have access to sufficient sources to be able to describe these movements in broad outline in Christendom at the end of the Middle Ages.[2] Philippe Contamine has used the work of Hugues Neveux on the Cambrai region to provide the following indices of production for oats and wheat:

Oats:
c. 1320: 160–70
c. 1370: 100
c. 1450–60: 65–70
c. 1520: 80

Wheat:
c. 1320: 140–50
c. 1370: 100
c. 1450–80: 80
c. 1520: 90–5

These falls were certainly primarily a consequence of the demographic collapse.

During the same period, however, industrial prices remained fairly stable. This led Contamine to the conclusion that there had been an unequal division of profits between agricultural regions and industrial regions. Julien Demade, on the basis of a series of bread prices for Nuremberg between 1427 and 1538,[3] has demonstrated in great detail the two main types of price variability, intra- and inter-annual, and shown how great both of them were. The introduction of money into the fixing of prices and into the sale of numerically valued foodstuffs brings out a fact to which I have already drawn attention but which has been generally neglected, the repercussions of monetary circulation on the period. Demade also observed that, especially in southern Germany, the monetary levies demanded by the dominant from the dominated were concentrated in time, coming soon after the harvests, but with a time lag sufficient for the latter to sell their produce. This price variation reveals both the link between the market in foodstuffs and seigneurial taxation and the role of time in the functioning of medieval society, in the sphere of prices as elsewhere.

This is the point to observe that, in the words of Demade, 'the emergence and growth of the market at the end of the Middle Ages had nothing to do with some putative transition to capitalism; on the contrary, it amounted to a new organization of the feudal system which greatly strengthened it.' True, this was a part of Europe which, as demonstrated by the fine Polish historian Marian Malowist, remained underdeveloped to the point of experiencing a second serfdom in the fifteenth century, which was most pronounced in the most easterly regions, such as Hungary and Poland, where monetary circulation was on a very small scale.[4] However, the link between the market in foodstuffs and seigneurial taxation was visible everywhere in the West at the end of the Middle Ages. I will go further, and quote the words of Laurent Feller: 'Buying and selling were not prompted by trading considerations alone but also obeyed social logics, themselves determined by kinship, friendship and neighbourhood as well as by adherence to a particular group of equivalent status.'[5] I repeat, apart from these social solidarities, the system of prices was also influenced by the growth of princely and urban bureaucracies and the efforts of institutions to levy taxes.

Wage movements

It will be helpful to compare these price movements with wage movements. Wages have often been presented as one of the principal factors in the destruction of the system we call feudal. In reality, like money in general, wages were integrated without great difficulty into the operation of this system, and at a relatively early date – there were strikes aimed at obtaining higher wages in the 1260s. The transition from an estate system to a seigneurial system, in the context of the evolving feudal system, greatly expanded and accelerated the introduction of wages into the labour market. Bronislaw Geremek showed this in the urban context of late medieval Paris, but it was a general trend which greatly influenced the market in foodstuffs.

The demographic depression which followed the outbreak of the Black Death in 1348 led to a labour shortage which drove up wages between 1350 and 1450. The evidence for wages is particularly plentiful for the building trades and it has been put to good use in a study of the medieval mason in England.[6] For an English building worker, the wage index, which had been 94 in 1340–59, rose to 105 for the period 1360–79, and to 122 for the period 1380–99. Both the kings of England and the kings of France tried to limit these increases by statutes of labourers in 1361. They tried not only to return wages to what they had been in 1348, but also to prohibit the giving of alms to able-bodied beggars who refused to work, and in England even to put to work or to keep in work children aged twelve and above. Such regulation was extremely unpopular with craftsmen and workers and it seems to have been so difficult to enforce that it was eventually abandoned. In Upper Normandy, a skilled worker who had earned 2 sous tournois a day in 1320–40 saw his wages rise to 4 sous tournois between 1340 and 1405 and to 5 between 1405 and 1520. The wages of unskilled workers doubled during the period, the highest-known rise being that of the wages of porters in Wurzburg, which tripled.

A conference of European historians devoted to the subject of wages at the end of the Middle Ages was held in Barcelona in 2007. It showed that, as is well known, or as might have been expected, there were big differences between the wages of different workers, with master craftsmen, including in the building trades, and more generally those performing tasks of organization and direction, being better paid, and also that wage differentials, from apprentice to master, increased. Hours of work were regulated by statute, a sign of the influence of payment in cash on the conception and use of time. In Pistoia, for example, the hours of work were different in summer and winter, the unit of working time was twenty minutes and wages were cut if workers turned up late. At the end of the Middle Ages, a special and higher wage meant that architects, painters and sculptors moved from the category of craftsmen to the status of artists. As emphasized by Henri Bresc (in an electronic book on work in the Middle Ages), the increase in the use of cash on building sites and in manual labour also affected another concept which medieval people, from theologians to the poor, found difficult to grasp and define, that of work.

The growth of luxury

In spite of all the miseries and hardships of the late fourteenth and the fifteenth centuries, in particular war and epidemics, luxury, which had already been expanding in the thirteenth century, spectacularly increased, tempting the upper ranks of seigneurial and bourgeois society into increasingly lavish expenditure. Throughout this period, governments, and especially kings and towns, attempted to restrain this upward surge in expenditure. The Church did the same for religious reasons, although a monument like the Palace of the Popes in Avignon reveals that the papacy was one of the biggest institutional spenders in the West, if not the biggest of all, though less for personal pleasure than as a collective assertion of prestige. After Philip the Fair, John the Good in 1355–6 and Charles V in 1366 condemned various types of luxury expenditure, such as jewels and large items of gold or silverware. Charles V also, as we have seen, prohibited the wearing of the extravagant pointed shoes *à la poulaine*. In 1367, he specifically prohibited the women of Montpellier from wearing precious stones or – immorality here added to opulence – clothes that were too low-cut. In 1485, Charles VIII forbade fabrics of silk or velvet. Italy was especially anxious to restrict these excesses of splendour, which can be seen as more of a Renaissance than a strictly medieval phenomenon.

Luxury at table was particularly condemned. In fact, money encouraged the development of many capital sins, which only reinforced the Church's negative attitude towards it. *Avaricia* (avarice) was often promoted to first place among the capital sins. *Gula* (gluttony), which had been fiercely attacked by monastic asceticism in the Early Middle Ages, and then seemingly become acceptable with the development of 'table manners' in the thirteenth century, was condemned afresh in the fourteenth and fifteenth centuries. Public opinion, which was beginning to emerge as a phenomenon, was caught between two opposing sentiments with regard to such luxury and the expenditure it entailed. On the one hand, it supported the hostility of the Church and popular hostility to the 'new rich'; on the other, it saw it as a mark of prestige in a society based on a profound inequality of social categories. The fourteenth and fifteenth centuries were the age of banquets that both dazzled people and shocked them. In this form of luxury, too, money both fuelled and aggravated the contradictory effect of hierarchy in feudal society. It encouraged the battle between condemnation and admiration in *mentalités*.[7] Luxury contributed to the growth of indebtedness, created in large part by the monetization of the economy and one of the great plagues of the fourteenth and fifteenth centuries.

The fifteenth century was thus one of oppositions in which money seems to have played an ever-increasing role. We are now justified in speaking of a category of new rich, marked by an increasingly ostentatious luxury which was particularly visible in more lavish furniture and the success of tapestry; the towns, meanwhile, were swarming with increasing numbers of poor. This was the age of the Paris of Villon, the capital of 'beggars'.

The diversity of coins at the end of the Middle Ages

What was the state of monetary circulation in Europe around 1400? Peter Spufford has tried to answer this question, and I draw heavily on his work for what follows. We need to remember that there were three distinct monetary levels: the highest level, that of gold; a middling level, primarily characterized by silver coins; and lastly the lowest level of billon or 'black' money, usually of copper. At the two higher levels, there was a tendency for both an increase in the circulation of coins and a reduction in the types of coins in use. The former was due to the recovery of trade and expansion of public and private life, the latter to the growth of princely monopolies over coinage and the domination of certain financial networks. The consequence was a trend towards the formation of relatively 'national' monetary systems and the strengthening of the circulation of the two great 'international' currencies, the florin of Florence and the ducat of Venice. In the fifteenth century, the Venetian ducat acquired a position of such dominance that it replaced the term 'florin'. Its influence was also felt on the content in precious metal and weight of the other principal European gold coins. The gold écu of France was reduced in 1424 to the same weight as the florin. In 1412, the English gold noble became a double florin or ducat. The prestige of gold coins in fifteenth-century Europe made the ducat a sort of standard. The coins minted with the gold brought back from Africa by the caravels of the Portuguese Henry the Navigator in the mid-fifteenth century were called cruzados and they were of the same weight and fineness as the ducat. Gold was particularly associated with the large payments typical of war, fertile territory for the use of money, and especially with the payment of princely ransoms. The ransom of the king of France, John II the Good, the dowry of Isabella of France, bride of Richard II of England, the ransom of James I of Cyprus and the price of the abandonment by John of Gaunt of his rights to the Castilian throne were all paid in ducats.

The value of these gold coins was so high that the vast majority of the medieval population never used them. Gold coins were for noblemen, high-level administrators and great merchants. When the new Dutch gold cavalier was put into circulation in 1433, it was worth 72 gros. The following year, in Antwerp, the master masons building the church of Notre Dame were paid at 8 gros per day and their journeymen at 4½ gros. In the countryside, the wages of agricultural workers were even lower. For the majority of the population, the most important coins were the silver coins they used for their everyday payments: wages, rents and taxes.

In the kingdom of France, the key coin in use from the second half of the fourteenth century was the 'blanc', which weighed around 3 grams and contained a little less than 50 per cent silver. Its silver content was therefore only about one third of that of its pre-Hundred Years War equivalent, the gros called 'argent le roi', which had been almost pure silver. Imitations of the blanc were struck by semi-independent French princes such as the dukes of Brittany and Savoy. This blanc was stable for a very long time. The anonymous Bourgeois of Paris who kept a diary from 1405 to 1449 recorded the level of wages in blancs; it was also in blancs that he gave the prices of the products which made up most of his consumption: candles, oil, honey, vegetables and rare fruits. At a level above that of the 'black money' or billon used for minor daily transactions, the silver money used for products of better quality was called, by contrast, 'white money'.

In the four regions they brought together under their rule (Flanders, Brabant, Hainault and Holland), the dukes of Burgundy struck from 1433 a silver coin which played in these regions the role play by the blanc in the French kingdom, the patard. Like the blanc, the patard was used to pay for products of quality and rarely used by the poor. The chronicler Chastellain tells how the duke of Burgundy, Philip the Good, having got lost in a forest while hunting, was found by a woodcutter. Anxious to get home, the duke asked the woodcutter to take him to the main highway, promising him 4 patards, an amount which made the woodcutter exclaim in surprise. The duke then said that he unfortunately had no loose change on him, and asked the woodcutter to change a gold florin, which was clearly something the woodcutter had never seen before. The circulation of coins in accord with social importance thus presented the poor woodcutter with an almost miraculous gold coin. In northern Italy, the most advanced of the commercial regions of Europe, the richest town in the fifteenth century after Venice was Milan. The new silver coin struck by the Milanese in the middle of the fifteenth century, the silver half-pegione, replaced the grosso of St Ambrose, just as in France the blanc had replaced the gros tournois. The only major Italian city to remain independent of Milan was Venice, but the aftermath of the wars of the fifteenth century led to a series of depreciations of the Venetian grosso.

In general, the tendency throughout most of Europe in the fifteenth century was to favour a silver coin of middling value which suited the return to a middling level of economic activity, wage levels and tax payments.

For internal needs, the most solid coin in fifteenth-century Europe was certainly the English silver coin, the groat. Smaller denomination silver coins also circulated at this period, for example in Venice, where they were worth a shilling or twelve Venetian 'little pennies' (*denarii piccoli*); these soldini were struck from 1328–9 and they soon became the principal coin for the payment of wages. Soldini were also struck in Florence and some found their way onto the Milanese market. At the very lowest level, the little pennies, or black money, circulated mainly in the regions with large towns where a part of the population lived on the edge of poverty and made only limited use of these coins. This was the case with the towns of the Low Countries, with Paris and London, and above all in northern Italy. This black money also seems to have been used in the large towns to pay for the services of prostitutes. Lastly, it was the mainstay of almsgiving and the Parisian denier or penny was called, as a result, the *denier de l'aumosnerie*. Oddly, the kings of England never had any black money struck in the fifteenth century. The people of London somehow managed to trade in products of small value without. However, for almsgiving they had to resort to other means, which meant that Venetian soldini which arrived in London through trade ended up being used for this purpose.

In transactions between Europe and the East, the Venetian ducat was by far the coin most used. In the East, even the Mamluks who ruled Egypt from 1425 struck ashrafi based on the ducat. The difference in value between superior gold, the silver used for normal transactions and the black money of daily exchanges was often very great. In Sicily, for example, in 1466, the gold reali were worth 20 good silver carlini, each of which was worth 60 black piccoli. The range was not generally so wide in Florence but the almost constant devaluation of the coins used to pay the textile workers (which they called *lanaiuoli*, that is, 'woolmen', after their employers) was one of the principal reasons for the social unrest which disturbed the town in the fourteenth century, and in particular during the famous revolt ('revolution') of the Ciompi in 1378–80. The worst problem for those who had to handle currencies was the constant instability of their value, which sometimes changed from one month to the next. The difference between the three levels of currency in circulation in Venice was less great, due to the exploitation of the silver mines of nearby Serbia. In 1413, the ducat was worth 124 soldini, which meant that there was a much narrower gap between denominations than in Sicily or Florence. It will be helpful here to quote the judicious remarks of the great historian of the economy, and in particular of money, Jean Meuvret, on the subject of some observations made by the Bourgeois of Paris in his *Journal* in 1421: 'Only a small part of the population, such as merchants and financial administrators, were familiar with gold coin. The people in general used silver coins for major purchases alone, the only current money being billon or fractional money; most needs were satisfied by home production, the closed economy or barter.'[8]

These views have often been criticized, judged applicable to the sixteenth century but not to the fifteenth. I am myself in agreement with Meuvret, who believed that the situation was the same in the fifteenth century. On the other hand, for payments or valuations of any importance, silver coins circulated not only among the middling classes in towns, for example for wages or rents, but also among the peasantry, who usually received silver coin for the part of their own harvest that they sold.

In 1469, Louis XI, Edward IV, Frederick III, Charles of Burgundy and envoys from Venice met in conference to try to define clearly the relationships between the various currencies. This followed from an awareness on the part of the most powerful political leaders of the monetary disorder, and perhaps threat of a monetary famine, especially in black money, both of which historians today regard as one of the principal brakes on medieval 'lift off'.

Appendix: Was There a Land Market in the Middle Ages?

The question of whether there was a unified market in the whole of Christendom in the Middle Ages is crucial to a definition of the nature of the economy, and more particularly the monetary economy that is our concern here. Given the importance of the rural economy in medieval societies, and following the publication of works on this subject, in particular those of Chris Wickham in the 1990s, French medievalists have taken up the theme. Chief among them have been Laurent Feller and François Menant, and a collection of articles jointly edited by Feller and Wickham, and dealing with the whole of Europe, was published in 2005, with the title *Le Marché de la terre au Moyen Age* (*The Land Market in the Middle Ages*). Not all the views expressed in this book point in the same direction. In any case, the problematic is influenced by the fact that the word 'market', as generally understood, is more characteristic of the English than the French historiography.[9]

The conclusion to what is an immensely valuable volume, although leaving many important questions open, tends rather in the direction of the absence of a land market in the Middle Ages, a view forcefully argued at a more general level by Alain Guerreau.[10] The nature of this research makes reference to anthropology imperative, and Monique Bourin points out in the Preface that most of the contributors have distanced themselves from the views of Karl Polanyi, previously most frequently cited, in favour of those of Chayanov (1888–1939). From the ideas of Chayanov deemed applicable to the medieval economy has come a conception of a peasant economy in which the problematic of the land market has incorporated the idea that transactions are dominated, or at least largely determined, by the cyclical evolution of the size of the landholdings according to that of families. This thesis has influenced in particular the majority of the English-speaking historians who have studied the question of the existence of a land market in the majority of peasant economies at all periods. I myself believe, on the contrary, as I argue elsewhere in this book, that Polanyi was correct in thinking that, before the Industrial Revolution in Europe, as in the rest of the world, the domination of the economic over the social was unknown, economic phenomena being, in any case, themselves inseparable from their social context.[11]

I share, I repeat, the views expressed by Monique Bourin in her Preface (p. xi), where she observes that there were regions and periods in the Middle Ages where land transactions were imbricated into the fabric of social relations, power relations and hierarchies that generally corresponded to reality. Laurent Feller is right to refer, as the starting point in French historiography of consideration of the uses peasants made of land, to the book by Henri Mendras, *La Fin des paysans*, first published in 1967 (with a new edition in 1991). Here Mendras argued that, before being a tool of production, land was for the medieval peasant an affective possession with which he had a special relationship. In her work on land transactions in Spain, and in particular Galicia, Reyna Pastor has shown that the sale of a piece of land was often a form of exchange which relates back to a gift economy concealed behind a fiction, that of the economic character of the transaction in question.

Feller concludes his survey by observing that land transfers in the Middle Ages have to be described with reference to mechanisms not all of which obey the laws of the market. He emphasizes the importance of social and familial solidarities, and the fact that these transactions could have taken the form of gifts but, by choice of the actors, are made using money (p. 28). Florence Weber argues that the market relationship occupies a narrow territory between war and interpersonal alliance. And although they are applied to an earlier period, the tenth and eleventh centuries, the ideas of the American medievalist Barbara Rosenwein,[12] which have much influenced historians working on Cluny in the Middle Ages, show that many other motives, non-economic and non-monetary, inspired the monks of the Cluniac order: generosity and eschatological thinking, asceticism and communion with the monastic ideal, the activation and maintenance of networks of alliances and the protection of family patrimonies by the endowment of the children entering monasteries. In short, as emphasized by Patrice Beck in *Le Marché de la terre*, these land transactions originated in the gift economy and persisted long after the eleventh century of Cluny. In his work on the county of Vendôme, Dominique Barthélemy[13] showed how transactions involving land combined a gift economy and a market economy. It is this mix, based on the social relations within the seigneurie, which defines feudalism. While emphasizing the difficulty of comparing on the basis of different sources, in Spain where transactions were generally made via a notary, and England, where the aristocratic and ecclesiastical archives contain little numerical information, Carlos Laliena Corbera makes two points necessary to any discussion of the land market in Spain in the Late Middle Ages: it was a very fragmented market, both on the regional and the local scale, and it was a market in which personal, non-economic factors played an important role (clientism and family ties, in particular) (p. 182).

François Menant, in his fine chronological study of the appearance of discussion of the land market in the various European historiographies, notes that it predates the great works on the economy of rural society in France and in England (such as those of Georges Duby, Robert Fossier and André Chédeville for France and Michael Postan for England) and also that this theme, combined with the influence of Chayanov, has been prominent in England but remained external to the work of French and Italian historians. Only the English historian Chris Wickham has introduced it into his studies of the rural economy of Italy in the Middle Ages. In France, only certain historians of the *Annales* school and a few others in Italy, such as Giovanni Levi, practitioners of *microstoria*, have tackled this theme. In Spain, the subject of the land market was introduced at a late stage, and the emphasis has been on demonstrating its limits, to the extent of using the expression 'marketless transactions'.

Emanuel Grelois, discussing land transactions in Auvergne, notes that these transactions were more about the income, securities and rents inherent in this land than the land itself. He also notes the extreme unevenness of prices, even for areas of similar size, and concludes that in the fourteenth century, in spite of the very high level of monetization in the economy, land remained a reserve of value.

In his conclusion, Chris Wickham emphasizes that land transactions were always a mix of the economic and the social, and that this imbrication is characteristic of the feudal system, as was explained by the great Polish historian Witold Kula for another period and another country, Poland from the fifteenth to the seventeenth centuries, in his *Economic Theory of the Feudal System* (Warsaw, 1963) (there are French, English and Italian translations); Wickham also notes that, whatever the relative unity of the European feudal system in the Middle Ages, it was, as far as the land market was concerned, a system encompassing many regional and local differences.

13

The Mendicant Orders and Money

I return now to the much discussed and controversial question of the relationship between the mendicant orders – their very name a programme – and money. These orders, Dominican Preachers and Franciscan Minors, were founded in the thirteenth century. They were recognized by the pontifical hierarchy but operated free from episcopal control. They made it their mission to fight against heresy and, basing themselves closely on the example and words of Jesus Christ as contained in the New Testament, to maintain within Christian orthodoxy the new society which was emerging in Christendom, in particular in the towns. One of the principal problems they encountered was that of the relationship between this fundamental Christianity and the growth of activities that involved coin and what we today understand by the word 'money'.

From voluntary poverty to a market society?

In what can be described either as the battle against money or as the dialogue with it, it was the Franciscan order that was most deeply involved. Their founder, Francis of Assisi, was the son of a merchant. Fundamental to the theory and practice of his rebellion, aimed at achieving both his own salvation and that of others, was not only the battle against money but also the rejection of money. This led to the introduction into the order he founded, under pressure from the papacy, and to a lesser degree into the

Dominican order, the practice of begging, or mendicancy, hence the name that would be given to the brothers of these orders. St Francis and some of his companions hesitated between begging and manual labour as the basis of their existence, a hesitation that is beyond the scope of this study. What matters for us is the attitude of the mendicant orders to money, which throws light on the history that is the subject of this book; it has also given rise to a fierce debate in modern and contemporary historiography.

Francis of Assisi produced a first rule for the community of his brothers in 1221, on the orders of the papacy, which wanted these religious to form an order. The pope asked him to amend it, which he did, and in 1223 he drew up a new rule. This would be definitive, as it was confirmed by a pontifical bull. One of the chapters of the rule that was never operative consisted of a 'prohibition on the brothers receiving money', for which Francis used the words *pecuniam aut denarios* (money or coins); the brothers, it said, should take no more interest in these than they did in stones ('*quia non debemus maiorem utilitatem habere et reputare in pecunia aut denariis quam in lapidis*'). In the definitive rule, the clause concerning the abstention from money repeats the strict (*firmiter*) prohibition on receiving '*denarios vel pecuniam*' in any form, either directly or indirectly through the intermediary of another. It is much shorter, omitting the comparison between coins and stones, but the prohibition is still forcefully expressed.

I tried in my earlier book, *Your Money or Your Life*, to show how the thirteenth-century Church tried to reconcile for good Christians the use of money and the attaining of eternal salvation (life). The debate was primarily focused on the notion and practice of usury, which I discussed in this earlier book. I take the liberty of referring to it here because in it I defined the ideas which are crucial to this present study. The Middle Ages, I emphasized, had a very different view from our own of the realities which we today isolate and put into a specific category, 'the economic'. I quoted the great modern economist who was my principal inspiration for the avoidance of anachronism and the understanding of the functioning of 'the economic' in medieval society, Karl Polanyi (1886–1964), to whom I have already referred. I spoke in particular of how Polanyi showed that the economy, in certain ancient and medieval societies, 'was embedded in the labyrinth of social relations'. If I repeat this here, it is because it is equally applicable to the present study and because the ideas of Polanyi have been crucial in helping me to define what the men and women of the Middle Ages, including the theologians, believed in the sphere we today know as 'money'.

Many recent and contemporary historians believe that the mendicant orders, and in particular the Franciscans, starting from the notion of voluntary poverty, paradoxically developed a conception of money that would inspire the 'market society'.[1] I will confine myself here to emphasizing the weakness of the work on which Giacomo Todeschini, despite his great erudition, essentially bases himself, that is, the *De emptionibus et venditionibus* of Peter John Olivi, to whom I have also already referred. Olivi was a very controversial figure, and I am among those who believe that this marginal treatise had little influence in the Middle Ages and, further, that it represents the extreme end of a spectrum of atypical thinking, rather than a generally accepted view.

What is certain, and important, is that the Franciscans founded credit agencies intended to provide the minimum amount of money necessary for many poor people to survive, but only at the end of the fifteenth century. The new poverty remained to the end of the Middle Ages one of the essential objectives of the mendicant orders, and particularly the Franciscans. Daniela Rando has defined the *mont-de-piété* (mount of piety) as 'an institution created with the intention of providing short-term loans to the urban working classes in return for the guarantee of a security and payment of moderate interest'.[2] The oldest recorded foundation of this type was in Perugia, in 1462, on the initiative of the Franciscan Michele Carcano of Milan. This institution spread throughout northern Italy and then all over Europe. The creation of a *mont-de-piété* generally followed preaching by a brother, usually a Franciscan. The institution was organized by the urban authorities, who put together an initial capital through collections, gifts, legacies and so on, appointed directors and drew up operating rules. Those behind the *monts-de-piété* tried to ensure that the loans were made freely, but the best they could manage was to maintain the interest rates at a very low level, around 5 per cent. The *monts-de-piété* were fiercely criticized because they were seen by some as a form of usury, which shows how the practice of usury and the debate surrounding it persisted to the end of the Middle Ages. Pope Leo X, by the bull *Inter multiplices*

(1515), brought the controversy to an end by legitimizing the *monts-de-piété*.

The accounting practices of the mendicant orders

Given that the ideas and practices of the mendicant orders in the sphere of money have assumed such importance, I would like to close this section by referring to the remarkable symposium organized by Nicole Bériou and Jacques Chiffoleau on the subject of 'Economy and Religion: The Experience of the Mendicant Orders from the Thirteenth to the Fifteen Century'.[3] Drawing on the conclusions of Jacques Chiffoleau, I would like to emphasize the distinctiveness of the practices of the mendicant orders, in particular the Franciscans, in relation to the innovations introduced by certain emergent groups among the laity in the sphere that would later be called the economy. These new practices derived from a certain rationalization of the Christian life as a whole, as noted by Max Weber, and were adopted by the old monasteries, the cathedral chapters or canons, episcopal households and, most of all, the papacy itself before the mendicant orders. The latter were not as innovative in this sphere as has sometimes been claimed.

In this context in particular, as emerged clearly from a round table held in Rome in 2003, the Apostolic Camera itself did not unify its various accounting procedures.[4] In using these new systems, the Franciscans always gave priority to the principle of voluntary poverty which was their main message. In fact, the accounting practices of the mendicants, in the words of Jacques Chiffoleau, now seem to us cruder than those of the specialists in trade or taxation.[5] They consisted, in essence, of 'regularly checking the state of their poverty by noting their expenditure on food and clothing and their debts against unpredictable gifts and the regular rents they could count on'. In the face of the new management techniques emerging during 1360–80, the mendicants continued to be primarily oriented towards what Max Weber called 'the economy of salvation'. The financing of the mendicant churches and convents, which proliferated in the fourteenth century, came primarily from gifts *pro mortuis*, legacies and requests to be buried in their churches or cemeteries, as we have already observed with regard to the construction and decoration of the chapel of the Scrovegni in Padua, described in the fine book of Chiara Frugoni. This was a very different type of behaviour from that of the rich laymen and women who invested their money in building. To use once again the words of Jacques Chiffoleau,

> the magnificent churches and rich buildings of the mendicants of the Late Middle Ages did not contravene the rules of life of the brothers as much as has been claimed, for the simple reason that these buildings and their furnishings were never completely in their hands. The mendicant convent could not be a place that belonged to the brothers alone.

All over Europe, the income of the mendicant orders came primarily from *rentes constituées*, a sort of annuity created by the urban or princely authorities as a way of managing the public debt. They were therefore an aspect of the safeguarding of the common good rather than the property of either the brothers or the city or princely authorities. The word *pensio*, which was used for all these revenues of the brothers, puts the emphasis on the fact that it was above all the provision of *victum et vestitum* (food and clothing) that was at issue, which was not contrary to the practice of poverty. Further, as the use or usufruct of the annuities and rents was received by the mendicants through the intermediary of procurators, they could claim to be at arm's length from the ownership and management of property, which did not always convince the critics among their contemporaries – or some historians today. It is interesting that the need to make use of lay intermediaries for certain operations that would be contrary to their vows of voluntary poverty may have drawn the brothers more deeply into ordinary urban activities than their preaching, and increased the effectiveness of their pastoral mission in the towns. This is just one example of the role of money in the Middle Ages and of its impact on the formation of societies and social groups. Money established or at least strengthened links between those who used it – links that might not otherwise have existed. In the fourteenth and fifteenth centuries, the resort to the Franciscans, especially for burial in their convents and for their prayers for the dead, accounted for nearly half the order's income. Death was monetarized. The developing belief in the existence of Purgatory also encouraged gifts in money, even quite small, made through the intermediary of a collection box or 'Purgatory alms-bowl' of the sort found in most churches. It is useful to recall here that as early as the beginning of the twelfth century Honorius Augustodunensis had said that the consecrated host was like a coin necessary to salvation, a metaphor evidently suggested by the shape of the host, showing that it was not what we today call money that mattered in the Middle Ages, but rather the coins that circulated widely with different names, values and origins, which had become a new way of life.

In the fourteenth and fifteenth centuries, the notion of voluntary poverty came up against the valorization of the notion of work and a growing condemnation of the able-bodied beggar, as opposed to the mendicant orders, voluntary poor who begged increasingly less often.

As I try to show in this book, at the heart of the economy of salvation and its social functioning were 'mercy, *caritas* and the gift'. The symposium on 'Economy and Religion' referred to above also showed that, contrary to the views of Alain Guerreau, the Middle Ages were familiar with the idea of risk and that the mendicants themselves included the existence, in certain circumstances, of risk in their vision of human activity. I am less convinced by the final claim to the effect that historians make too sharp a distinction between the history of religion and that of the economy. The evolution of the relationship between the mendicant orders, in particular the Franciscans, and what we today call the monetary economy shows that it is mistaken to separate religion and economy in the Middle Ages; the latter – and here I repeat the arguments of Polanyi – was always incorporated into the activities of human beings dominated and wholly inspired by religion. It is to my mind an error on the part of excellent historians such as Giacomo Todeschini to have assumed a virtual economic thinking among the Franciscans. It is true that the teaching and behaviour of the Church included precepts and practices which had an impact on what we today call the economy, but as the latter was not only not recognized but did not exist, the conceptions and behaviour of the Franciscans had a different significance and other goals. Voluntary poverty was not economic in character. Nor do I think that it can be limited to an ethic. It was more a way of thinking and above all of behaving before God in the spheres in which the Bible and tradition had taught Christians how they ought to conduct themselves so as to avoid attracting

God's wrath. It is this behaviour, which involved social status and position among the Christian people, that we need to examine in order to discover whether this reading and this use of the Church's teaching could allow a place for money, or if money was no more than simply an element – not always clearly perceived – of wealth. I continue to believe that, even if the word 'rich' was increasingly often used, the medieval conception was essentially still that of the early medieval dichotomy between the powerful and the poor. Some religious movements, especially the mendicant orders, in order to emphasize the spirit and terms in which they approached the problem, introduced the expression 'voluntary poverty', alongside the traditional term 'poverty'. It was not an economic attitude that was expected of the voluntary poor but a way of living and thinking.

14

Humanism, Patronage and Money

As we have seen, the Church, the principal economic power in Europe since the Early Middle Ages, had adapted without great difficulty to the increase in the circulation of money, especially from the thirteenth century. I have paid particular attention to the relationship between money and the mendicant orders, especially the Franciscans, because they have been since their emergence in the thirteenth century the focus of a fierce debate about the role and value of money, which is still alive today in their historiography. While it is essential to recognize differences between the various ecclesiastical milieus, and over time in the attitudes of the Church in general, of the Holy See in particular, and of the monastic and mendicant milieus, it can still be said that the Christianity incarnated in these various sectors of the Church was in general fairly hesitant about, and even hostile to, money. Given that the Church was the dominant power in every sphere of medieval life, its mistrustful attitude to money influenced not only the thinkers but also ordinary men and women in their daily lives, at least until the fourteenth century. In the fourteenth and fifteen centuries, European Christians moved on and, in the eyes of some historians, there was a transformation in their attitude to money. Whilst I myself doubt that the definition of the rich man changed fundamentally at this period, or that wealth came to be equated with money, I cannot deny that such a change happened in the case of the tiny cultural and social elite which appeared at the end of the Middle Ages and which we call the humanists. I believe that the essential starting point for this psychological and cultural shift was the change in the attitude to merchants. The Church had accepted merchants, initially doomed to Hell, at a very early date, mainly by recognizing their utility, and on condition they respected certain values which can in the thirteenth century be summed up as the requirement for justice. André Vauchez has shown that the slow process of rehabilitating the merchant, which was completed at the beginning of the thirteenth century – the traditional proof being the canonization in 1199 of the merchant draper of Cremona, Homobonus, who died in 1197 – was a first step towards the conversion of the Church to respect for 'business' and consequently increasingly for money.[1]

A first humanism

The transition was often far from clear between wholehearted condemnation by the Church of all the attitudes linked to commercial and banking practices, and categorized as usury, and that of practices which were simply associated with the sin of greed, *avaritia*, one of the seven capital sins since the twelfth century but which changed gradually into tolerance and then, among some proto-humanists, into a eulogy of wealth, including monetary wealth.

Nicole Bériou has shown that there were 'variations' on the love of money among thirteenth-century preachers, which she has described in her fine study of 'the spirit of lucre between vice and virtue'.[2] They combated the spirit of lucre in various ways, sometimes by traditional images, such as that of St Martin giving half his cloak to the poor beggar Damian. Usury was often treated as a form of theft, an idea already employed by St Ambrose and then repeated in the mid-twelfth century by the Decretum of Gratian. The preachers often condemned the evil rich by reference to the harm they did to the poor, those new heroes of thirteenth-century Christianity. The usurers were castigated as murderers of the poor. However, Nicole Bériou has emphasized that 'it did not occur to the preachers, any more than to the theologians, to see the economy as a subject of investigation that might be studied for its own sake.' Their objectives were religious in kind, and lucre appears as a sin, or at least as one of the weaknesses of human nature. The life of the Christian was not measured by the yardstick of money; what the preachers emphasized in this century was that the love of God was free.

This attitude of the early humanists to money was not immediately articulated in the fourteenth century. Indeed, Patrick Gilli has shown that the humanists of this period usually shared the hostile attitudes to money of the fiercest critics of monetary wealth among the Franciscans. Their positions were even often backward by comparison with the relative tolerance of St Thomas Aquinas, who had recognized wealth, including monetary wealth, as making a small but real contribution to Man's fulfilment on earth. This hostility to money is found, most notably, in Petrarch, who declared in his treatise *Remedies for Fortune Fair and Foul*, written in the years 1355–65, that 'Love of money is the sign of a mean spirit.' Of the thinkers of Antiquity to whom these humanists liked to refer, it was Seneca, Stoic enemy of money, that they mostly quoted. However, there was a change, perhaps even a turning point, early in the fifteenth century. The first open defence of the benefits of wealth for mankind is found in a Venetian humanist, the patrician Francesco Barbaro, in his treatise on marriage, *De re uxoria*, written in 1415. However, the true turning point in the attitude of the humanists to money came not so much in Venice, important though the latter was in the process, but in Florence. Leonardo Bruni, philosopher and man of government, praised wealth in the preface to his Latin translation (1420–1) of the *Economics* of the pseudo-Aristotle, dedicated to Cosimo de Medici. The culmination of the new thinking came in the *De avaritia* of the Florentine Poggio Bracciolini around 1429 and then and above all in the *Books on the Family* of the great architect and theoretician of art, Leon Battista Alberti, dated to the years 1437–41. Alberti had studied in Venice and Padua. More importantly, he belonged to a great Florentine family and was very close to Brunelleschi, the famous builder of the dome of Florence cathedral. In his treatise, Alberti goes so far as to claim: 'We see that money is the root, the lure and the nourishment of everything. No one can be in doubt that money is the spirit behind all the crafts, so that he who has plenty of it can escape all necessities.' We should not forget, however, just how extreme these views of Alberti were, or that these new standard-bearers for money represented an elite or, rather, a minority. We may see as more common not only in ecclesiastical circles but in the business world too the views of Giordano of Pisa, following in the footsteps of Thomas Aquinas, expressed in one of the sermons he delivered in Florence in the fourteenth century:

> Aristotle says that there are two types of rich man, one natural, the other artificial. The natural one is comparable to the wealth of the fields and the vineyards which provide a living for he who cultivates them and for his family. These are the finest type of rich man, those who incur no blame. And many cities are radiant with this wealth. The other rich men, who are called artificial, are those who manufacture products and who make money from this. The cities are full of them too, but most of them do not avoid usury, and these are the worst rich men. To become rich like this, men become shameful, wicked, traitorous and corrupt.

The Albertis and the Brunis notwithstanding, the Middle Ages did not love money. There may be an element of truth in the ideas of Max Weber, however questionable, regarding the relationship between Protestantism and money but it is in my view more a question of date than of internal relationships. The sixteenth century was the century of the Reformation and, as we will see, the first beginnings of capitalism.[3]

Patronage

If there is one area of human life where the ideas and the behaviour of medieval people differed fundamentally from our own, it is surely that of art. As is well known, the word 'art' only acquired its present meaning in the nineteenth century (from the German *Kunst*), and the word 'artist' only finally split off from the word 'artisan' at the end of the eighteenth century, when the distinction between the 'mechanical arts' and the 'liberal arts', which simply continued the ancient usage, disappeared.

However, the absence of these ideas did not prevent men of power in the Middle Ages from commissioning what we today call works of art from creators we today call artists. The construction of the most spectacular buildings – churches and castles – was long seen as a product of religious feeling, and of a desire to honour God, and these buildings as the work of devout Christians, who laboured with their own hands or obliged free and servile peasants to labour on their behalf; castles were similarly assumed to have been built by the labour owed by subjects to their lord. It has long been known that, with very limited and rare exceptions, this was not the case. I have already referred to the fine study in which the American Henry Kraus showed that the building of the cathedrals was extremely expensive, due to the purchase of the stone and the wages of the architects and labourers. It seems to me, however, that, especially from the twelfth century, with the replacement of wood by stone and the refinement of painting and above all sculpture, one of the sectors responsible for the greatest increase in expenditure, and hence need for money, was what we call patronage. We should not forget that, as Umberto Eco has shown, the notion of beauty was slow to develop in the Middle Ages, and that, if merchants were particularly prominent among the patrons, it was primarily so as to demonstrate their enhanced social status, even more than their wealth; less monumental works of art often became commodities. A particularly well-studied example is that of Avignon in the fourteenth century, when the residence there of the popes and cardinals, with their entourages, made it a market in rare books, paintings and tapestries.

However, we should not forget, as Marc Bloch showed, that the owners of works of art had no hesitation, in case of need, or if the fancy seized them, in melting them down in order to recover the precious metal; though marginal to economic life, this testifies to the lack of interest of medieval people in what was regarded as no more than manual labour. It is true that, with the approach of the Renaissance, patronage grew to such an extent that, even though economic activity had not yet acquired the pre-capitalist character sometimes attributed to it, those we call bankers, and especially the Italians, no longer demanded from their commercial success a prestige they now sought from their political activity or their patronage. The most outstanding example of this was undoubtedly that of the Medici, a family whose first costly funerary monument was the marble sarcophagus of Giovanni di Bicci de Medici, who died in 1429; his great-grandson Lorenzo the Magnificent (1449–92) is now famous not as a banker but as a politician and a patron.

A market in luxury

Perhaps even more than patronage, it was the growth of luxury that caused people to feel a need for money. In the fifteenth century, there was a revival of the sumptuary laws which tried, though without much success, to restrict this splendour. Italy, and Florence in particular, was then a major producer of wedding caskets and chests in which young brides kept their trousseaus and their presents. Above all, the fifteenth century was the century of tapestry. In this case, it was Flanders and the Low Countries which were dominant, in towns like Arras, Lille and Brussels. Despite the efforts of the Church, and in particular the reformed mendicant orders, the Observants, the growth of luxury was encouraged, as we have seen, by the new literary tastes and the new *mentalités*. The end of the medieval period was the age of the first humanists. In spite of the spread of luxury and of the taste for it, the fifteenth century saw a new crop of the sumptuary laws which had first appeared at the end of the thirteenth century, with the emergence of the new lovers of luxury; they were now not so much the lords as the wealthy burgesses, and especially their wives.

An interest in the subject of money always leads on to social history. The fifteenth-century sumptuary laws were not in general aimed at particular social categories, as had still been the case with certain statutes of the Italian towns in the fourteenth century; rather, they were aimed at society as a whole. A particularly interesting case is the sumptuary legislation of Count Amadeus VIII of Savoy who, during the upheavals which marked the end of the Great Schism, became pope from 1439 to 1449 under the name of Felix V. The statutes of Amadeus VIII of 1430 probably express the philosophy of the many governments, kings, princes and communes who introduced similar regulations. They went beyond the desire to moderate expenditure and the use of money. They were a veritable code of good conduct for the subjects of a prince or an institution. They decreed, for example, the abolition of prostitutes and they cracked down harshly on blasphemers, who were blamed for all the ills of the period – plague, storms, earthquakes and famine. The restrictions imposed on the use of money were adapted to a social hierarchy which had the duke at the top and the peasants at the bottom. The regulation of dress, which was central to these laws, did not apply only to the type of clothes, but also to accessories, to the quality of the fabrics, to furs, to the cut of the garments and, of course, to headgear. Finery, jewellery and the use of gold and silver were all strictly supervised. Attitudes which are for us a matter of fashion were then seen in terms of morality, the length of clothes, in particular, depending on position in the hierarchy, the long taking precedence over the short. Every aspect of the life of the people of Savoy was circumscribed and supervised by these statutes, especially marriages, burials and banquets. Two clauses were devoted to the penalties and fines imposed for failure to comply. It has been suggested that the severity of these measures, even if they were not enforced in full, might have had some influence, over the long term, on the mentality of the Savoyards and of the inhabitants of what is today western Switzerland. Was Amadeus VIII, with his sumptuary laws, the precursor of John Calvin?[4]

The objects which illustrate the growth of a market in luxury items in the fourteenth and fifteenth centuries included Parisian ivories, alabasters of Nottingham, copperware and the tapestries of Arras. Jacques Coeur was only one of those who traded in objets d'art. The great Florentine burgesses organized a competition for the decoration of the doors of the baptistery. This external luxury provoked a degree of revolutionary vandalism, the most spectacular and most famous example probably being that of the Dominican Savonarola in Florence. The same pomp and the same taste for exotic, rare and costly products is visible in the transformation taking place in the fourteenth and fifteenth centuries in the culinary sphere, with the transition from cooking to gastronomy. Far more than the spices enjoyed by medieval lords, the new gastronomic luxury spread to wider sectors of society. The end of the Middle Ages was fond of its food and spent lavishly to satisfy this fondness. Among the most spectacular of these new and costly tastes were sugar and citrus fruits from the Mediterranean.

Among these new areas of expenditure in the fourteenth and fifteenth centuries, we should note the pilgrimage to the Holy Land, which had replaced the crusade for devout Christians since the Muslim reconquest of Palestine. One often essential element in the crusading spirit had been the desire to acquire through war, all the more so when it was holy, the land and property of others.

Pilgrimage should be seen from a diametrically opposed financial perspective: it cost money. This is what was written by the Italian pilgrim Mariano da Sienna in 1431, after his pilgrimage to the Holy Land: 'No one should go on a pilgrimage if he hasn't plenty of money.[5] If he does, he will be torn in two; either the other pilgrims will have to pay for him or he will have to deny his faith.'

15

Capitalism or *Caritas*?

A medieval absence: capitalism

Three major thinkers offered definitions of capitalism in the nineteenth and twentieth centuries. Their views have recently been discussed in a book of great interest by Philippe Norel.[1] Norel claims that, for Braudel, capitalism was very different from a market economy. It was a product of the emergence and increasing power of a group of merchants whose success was essentially based on provisioning the large towns in the face of the constraints of the political authorities. It was not so much a system of economic organization as a state of mind and a body of practices for bypassing regulation. For Braudel, the phenomenon had appeared by the twelfth century, at least in the Italian cities, and by the thirteenth century in Paris. Everything I have so far said in this book shows that I do not believe in the reality of this medieval capitalism.

For Karl Marx, still according to Norel, capitalism was a true mode of production. Its historical appearance came when the bourgeoisie and the nobility appropriated the modes of production. For Marx, though capitalist relations of production emerged very gradually between the twelfth and the fifteenth centuries, they were only truly established in the sixteenth and seventeenth centuries. For me, this view has at least the advantage of excluding the Middle Ages from capitalism. The third scholar discussed by Norel is Max Weber. In the early twentieth century, Weber defined capitalism as an organization of the economy aimed at the profit that could be made through the prior accumulation of a sufficient mass of capital. He believed that this system appeared in the sixteenth century, and became solidly established between the sixteenth and the nineteenth centuries. As is well known, Weber added a thesis which has been much debated, that of the influence exerted by the Protestant Reformation on, if not the birth, at least the growth of capitalism. The crux here for me in this argument is that it makes it impossible to speak of capitalism before the sixteenth century. We need to add to these three theses that of an American historian with close ties with Braudel, Immanuel Wallerstein. For Wallerstein, capitalism was linked to what Braudel called a world economy, and he saw Europe as joining a world economy around 1450, which makes this also the date of the birth of capitalism.

What are for me the essential components of capitalism which were not present in medieval Europe? The first is a sufficient and regular supply either of precious metals, making it possible to mint coins, or of paper money, as had already been achieved by the Chinese. As we have seen, the Middle Ages was several times on the brink of monetary famine, and this was still the case at the end of the fifteenth century. As is well known, Christopher Columbus among others, and perhaps first in his almost mystical conception of this El Dorado, for him Indian though in reality American, saw a land of gold that would satisfy the appetite of Christendom. The discovery of America meant the regular transfer to Europe of large quantities of precious metals, gold and silver, regulated in Europe by the Casa de Contrataciòn in Seville in the sixteenth century. It was only then that this first demand of capitalism was met.

A second precondition for the introduction of capitalism was the formation of a single market, in place of the multiplicity of markets which had fragmented the use of currencies, imperfectly regulated by the fairs and the Lombards. This happened only in the sixteenth century, and has still, for that matter, not been wholly achieved, through a succession of globalizations. The third component, which I see as decisive, is the appearance of an institution which failed to take root in Antwerp in the fifteenth century, but which was finally established in 1609 in Amsterdam, that is, the Stock Exchange.

The importance of *caritas*

I will now return to the historians who have denied the existence of capitalism, even of a pre-capitalism, in the Middle Ages, with whose ideas I largely agree, who look at the notion of value in the Middle Ages quite differently. I believe that we should accord a crucial role in this system to the notion of *caritas*, and that if we wish to define a type of economy to which we can relate the medieval monetary economy, we need to turn to the sphere of the gift.

Among medievalists, it is Anita Guerreau-Jalabert who seems to me to have best explained the importance of *caritas* and of the gift in western medieval society.[2] She argues that this society was dominated by religion and the Church, here agreeing with Polanyi, who emphasized that there was no such thing as an independent economy in the Middle Ages, but that it was imbricated into a whole dominated by religion. Money was not, therefore, an economic entity in the medieval West; its nature and its use were governed by other considerations. Guerreau-Jalabert notes that the god who dominated medieval society, according to the Epistle of John (5, 4, 8 and 16), was *caritas*, and that 'charity appears as the yardstick by which the quality of the Christian was measured. To act against charity was to act against God and sins against charity, it follows, were among the most serious.' It is easier to understand, seen from this perspective, why the practice in which money played an essential role, usury, was condemned as one of the worst of sins. She also explains that charity was not simply the supreme virtue for Christians. It was also the supreme 'western social value', which she demonstrates by quotations from Peter Lombard and Thomas Aquinas. Charity also, she adds, encompassed love and friendship, but though friendship, love, *caritas* and peace existed in ancient Rome, and still exist today, the realities encompassed by these words in the Middle Ages were not at all the same. They were 'different social logics', each of which had its own coherence. *Caritas* in general and money in particular, limited in the Middle Ages to coin, are, in the eyes of historians, associated within one same economic process. I repeat: the error of modern historians with regard to 'money' in the Middle Ages springs from their failure to pay attention to anachronism. *Caritas* was the essential social link between medieval man and God, and between all men in the Middle Ages. The point is several times made by Thomas Aquinas: 'Charity is the mother of all the virtues, inasmuch as it informs all the virtues' (*Summa theologica*, 1–2 q. 62, a.4).[3]

What sort of economy was it? Anita Guerreau-Jalabert clearly and convincingly shows that it was a form of gift economy, and that, in the social model of Christianity, 'the supreme gift is that of God's love for Man which puts Charity in hearts'. It is hardly surprising, therefore, that for her, as I have tried to show above, the essential act by which the use of money was justified in the Middle Ages was almsgiving. As almsgiving generally happened through the intermediary and under the control of the Church, we see once again the preponderance of the Church in the functioning of medieval society, including in the use of money. The spread of money in the Middle Ages should thus be seen as an extension of the gift. Jacques Chiffoleau has observed that an increase in commercial transactions and in the use of money at the end of the Middle Ages went together with an increase in voluntary gifts, which far exceeded the fiscal levies imposed by earthly powers.[4] Guerreau-Jalabert has returned, therefore, to the ideas of Polanyi: rather than speak of the economic thought of, for example, the scholastics, which did not exist, we should locate trade and material wealth firmly 'within a value system that was always subject to *caritas*'.

Alain Guerreau has shown that this shift of perspective with regard to monetary values also applied to the fixing of prices.[5] The 'just price', which reflected the ideas of the Church in this sphere, had three characteristics. The first was that it was defined locally, as was observed, for example, in the thirteenth century by the theologian Alexander of Hales. The just price was the price that was customary in a given place. The second characteristic was the stable nature, in keeping with the common good, of the prices used in transactions. It was, Guerreau observes, 'the exact opposite of what is usually understood by the notion of competition and the free play of supply and demand'. The third characteristic is the reference to *caritas*. Guerreau emphasizes that, in all the great theologians of the thirteenth century, William of Auvergne, Bonaventure and Thomas Aquinas, the notion of just price, which relates back to *justicia*, was, like it, based on *caritas*.

Together, these considerations mean that it is impossible to speak of capitalism, or even pre-capitalism, in the Middle Ages before the end of the fifteenth century. It was only in the sixteenth century that elements which would characterize capitalism appeared: the abundance of precious metals from America from the sixteenth century and the appearance of a lasting stock exchange, that is, according to the *Dictionnaire culturel*, 'an organized public market where transactions in values, commodities or services were carried out'.[6]

Elsewhere in this same dictionary, however, Alain Rey correctly notes that 'there was a radical change in western Europe towards the end of the eighteenth century', and he quotes an illuminating passage from an Enlightenment author, Guillaume-Thomas Raynal, in his *Philosophical History* of 1770 (III, 1). In other words, in spite of the important innovations of the sixteenth and seventeenth centuries, as I tried to show generally in a book with the title *A Long Middle Ages*,[7] we may also speak of 'a Long Middle Ages' in the case of the sphere we today refer to as money, one which lasted until the eighteenth century, which was also when the concept of economy first appeared.

I would like to observe here that, sometimes taken to extremes, even to excess, the ideas I have just expressed, and by which I am largely persuaded, appear in a work of great originality by a contemporary Spanish anthropologist, Bartolomé Clavero, published in Milan in 1991, and in French translation, with a preface which I contributed, in 1996.[8] This is a work which has caused much ink to flow. Clavero is primarily concerned with the period from the sixteenth to the eighteenth centuries but his book has an important introduction devoted to the Middle Ages with as starting point for the discussion medieval usury. For Clavero, all the historians of medieval usury and of its mental and practical environment have been on the wrong track. They have started from the contemporary world, and its phenomena, conceptions and vocabulary, and transported them to the Middle Ages, where they were unknown, did not operate and explain nothing. Their judgement has been clouded by anachronism, and in particular by the fascination of capitalism, fatal endpoint of economic thinking and practice, which, like a magnet, attracts medieval attitudes to what we call the economy. Clavero draws on various economists; first, as I do myself, on Polanyi, but also on Bernard

Groethuysen, E.P. Thompson and, in part, on Max Weber. Just as, for Clavero, the economy did not exist in the Middle Ages, so the law was not of overriding importance for the social order. Before it came charity, friendship, that is, 'mutual goodwill', and justice, but charity preceded justice. In the feudal world, the concept of benefit was first of all canonical, and over time became bank-related, but the bank, in the Middle Ages, was no more than a 'frontier practice'. The *antidora*, a word which in Greek meant benefit, signified the 'counter-gift', which came from the Bible and defined the relations between human society and God. Clavero explicitly says that 'the economy did not exist', but qualified this by adding 'but only an economy of charity'. In this system, the only event that can be compared with those of today is bankruptcy, and in fact most of the establishments that have been called banks in the Middle Ages failed. As for money, or rather moneys, 'currency was put at the service of the transmission of goods which was an expression of charity.' For me, what is probably most interesting in the work of Clavero is the criticism of most of our contemporaries, historians included, who are incapable of recognizing that the men of the past were different from us. An essential lesson from the study of money in the Middle Ages is the disastrous role of anachronism in historiography.

It has been a great pleasure to find the core of my ideas in the works of a contemporary economist who seeks to show that 'the Middle Ages could not be the age of the lift-off of capitalism,' adding: 'It was only in 1609, in Holland, that the drawing up of a balance sheet was required by Stevin, the first economist to be concerned with this type of rationalization'.[9]

Conclusion

According to Karl Polanyi, the economy had no specificity in western society until the eighteenth century. It was, he said, embedded in what he called the labyrinth of social relations.[1] I believe this observation to be equally true of the conceptions of the Middle Ages, which did not include the notion of economy, other than in the sense of domestic economy inherited from Aristotle, and I have tried in this book to show that this was true of money too. Money is notoriously difficult to define. As I indicated in my introduction, Albert Rigaudière has neatly demonstrated that the notion of money always eludes those who try to define it. The principal dictionaries bear witness to the difficulty of providing a precise definition: '[any sort of money] and by extension what this money represents: capital, funds, fortune, specie, cash, takings, resources, wealth, not counting colloquial expressions such as bread, dough, dosh...' (*Le Petit Robert*, 2003 edition).

This absence of a medieval notion of money has to be seen in conjunction with the absence not only of a specific economic sphere, but also of economic theses or theories. Historians who attribute an economic thought to scholastic theologians or to the mendicant orders, particularly the Franciscans, are guilty of anachronism. As a general rule, in most areas of individual or collective existence, medieval people behaved in ways that make them alien to us and which mean that contemporary historians need to turn to anthropology to inform their interpretations. This medieval 'exoticism' is particularly visible in the sphere of money. We have to substitute, for the general idea we have of it today, the medieval reality of many moneys, the minting, use and circulation of which expanded considerably in this period. It is difficult for us to appreciate the scale of this in the absence of adequate numerical sources from before the fourteenth century, and we are often ignorant of whether the money indicated in a source is metal coin or money of account.

The rise of money, especially from the twelfth century, during what Marc Bloch called the second feudal age, also permeated the institutions and practices we call feudalism. To oppose money and feudalism is to defy historical reality. The growth of money went together with the development of the whole of medieval social life. Though it was associated with the towns, money also circulated widely in the countryside. It benefited from the growth of trade, which is one of the reasons for the importance of the Italians in this sphere, including in northern Europe. The increasing use of money in the Middle Ages was also associated with the formation of princely and royal administrations, whose need for funds led to the creation, with varying degrees of success, of a range of taxes paid in cash. The greater presence of money in the Middle Ages took the form of a proliferation of currencies and it was only at a late stage, from the fourteenth century, and to a limited degree, that the use of these currencies was replaced by other means of exchange and of payment, such as the bill of exchange or the annuity. Further, even if the practice seems to have been less common at the end of the Middle Ages, types of thesaurization persisted, not only in the form of ingots but also and predominantly in the form of treasure and gold and silver objects.

It is also clear that, in parallel with a certain social and spiritual promotion of the merchant, the management of money benefited from a shift in the ideas and practices of the Church which, it seems, wished to assist the people of the Middle Ages in their desire to safeguard both their money and their lives, that is, both their earthly wealth and their eternal salvation. Given that, even in the absence of specific conceptions, a sphere like that of the economy existed outside any consciousness of it on the part of the clergy and the laity, or rather lack of consciousness of it, I remain inclined to locate the use of money in the Middle Ages within a gift economy, money sharing in the general subordination of human beings to the grace of God. Two conceptions seem to me to have dominated the use of money in the Middle Ages in earthly practice: the search for justice, most notably found in the theory of the just price, and the spiritual requirement expressed by *caritas*.

It may be true that the medieval Church, in the course of time, was induced to rehabilitate those who handled money, if only on certain conditions, and that in the late fourteenth and the fifteenth centuries, within a restricted elite consisting of those we call the pre-humanists, wealth – and particularly wealth in money – was restored to respectability. It remains the case that, though it may have ceased to be accursed and infernal, money remained suspect throughout the Middle Ages. Lastly, I feel I need to spell out, like many famous historians before me, that capitalism was not born in the Middle Ages, and that the Middle Ages was not even a pre-capitalist age: the shortage of precious metals and the fragmentation of markets prevented the necessary preconditions from being realized. It was only in the period between the sixteenth and the eighteenth centuries that there took place the 'great revolution' which Paolo Prodi wrongly situated, as I have tried to show, in the Middle Ages.[2] In the Middle Ages, money, like economic power, had not liberated itself from the global value systems of the Christian religion and society. The creativity of the Middle Ages lay elsewhere.

Notes

Introduction

1 Albert Rigaudière, in *L'Argent au Moyen Age*, Colloque of 1997 (Paris: Publications de la Sorbonne, 1998), p. 327.
2 Dante Alighieri, *Inferno*, Singleton trans. *The Divine Comedy*, Bollingen Series LXXX (Princeton, NJ: Princeton University Press, 1970), canto XVII, pp. 175–7.

Chapter 2 From Charlemagne to Feudalism

1 Jose E. Ruiz Domenec, 'Un "pauper" rico en la Cataluna carolingia a fines del siglo VIII', *Boletin de la Real Academia de Buenas Letras de Barcelona* 36 (1975–6), pp. 5–14.
2 There is a full and clear description of the manufacture of real coins in: Etienne Fournial, *Histoire monétaire de l'Occident médiéval* (Paris: Nathan, 1970), pp. 9–12; and an even better one in the more recent: Marie-Christine Bailly-Maître, *L'Argent. Du minerai au pouvoir dans la France médiévale* (Paris: Ed. Picard, 2002), with illustrations.
3 Stanislaw Suchodolski, 'Les débuts du monnayage en Pologne', *Revue suisse de numismatique* 51 (1972): 131–5.
4 Stéphane Lebecq, 'Aelfric et Alpert. Existe-t-il un discours clérical sur les marchands dans l'Europe du Nord à l'aube du XIe siècle?', *Cahiers de civilisation médiévale*, 26th year, nos 1–2 (Jan.–June 1984): 85–93.

Chapter 3 The Rise of Coin and Money at the Turn of the Twelfth and Thirteenth Centuries

1 Though assarting continued during the twelfth and thirteenth centuries, making it possible both to produce timber, which was often sold and hence a source of money, and to devote new areas to crops, with the possibility of new income. Bruno Lemesle, who has worked on the Anjou region, has emphasized what he calls the economic dynamism of the monasteries and shown how it led to frequent disputes between lords and monks.

2 Odette Chapelot and Paul Benoit (eds), *Pierre et métal dans le bâtiment au Moyen Age* (Colloque de Paris de 1982) (Paris: Editions EHESS, 1985), esp. L. Musset, 'La pierre de Caen: extraction et commerce XIe–XVe siècle', pp. 219–35.

3 The results of these excavations are published in *Archéologie des villages désertés: Dracy* (Paris: Armand Colin, 1970); see also Jean-Marie Pesez, 'L'habitation paysanne en Bourgogne médiévale', in the publication of the 1972 Colloque de Besançon: *La Construction au Moyen Age, histoire et archéologie* (Paris: Les Belles Lettres, 1973), pp. 219–37.

Chapter 4 The Glorious Thirteenth Century of Money

1 Jacqueline Caille, 'Les nouveaux ponts de Narbonne (fin XIIIe–milieu XIVe siècle). Problèmes topographiques et économiques', in *Hommage à André Dupont* (Montpellier: 1974), pp. 25–38.

2 Thomas M. Bisson, '*Confirmatio monete* à Narbonne au XIIIe siècle', in *Narbonne, archéologie et histoire* (Montpellier: 1973).

3 Alain Erlande-Brandenburg, *La Cathédrale* (Paris: Fayard, 1989), p. 276.

4 Andrea Giorgio and Stefano Moscadelli, *Costruire una cattedrale. L'opera di Santa Maria di Siena tra XII e XIV secolo* (Munich: Deutscher Kunstverlag, 2005).

5 Jean Gimpel, *Les Bâtisseurs de cathédrales* (Paris: Seuil, 1958), trans. Teresa Waugh as *The Cathedral Builders* (New York: Grove Press, 1983).

Chapter 5 Trade, Money and Coin in the Commercial Revolution of the Thirteenth Century

1 I have drawn heavily in this chapter on Peter Spufford's fine book, *Money and its Use in Medieval Europe* (Cambridge: Cambridge

University Press, 1988), although it is, in my view, too 'monetarist' in inspiration.

2 Translated into English by Dorothy Wyckoff: *Book of Minerals* (Oxford: Clarendon Press, 1967).

3 See the remarkable and illuminating book by Alexander Murray, *Reason and Society in the Middle Ages* (Oxford: Oxford University Press, 1978).

4 The following pages owe much to Marc Bompaire, in Philippe Contamine, Marc Bompaire, Stéphane Lebecq and Jean-Luc Sarrazin (eds), *L'Economie médiévale*, 3rd edn (Paris: Armand Colin, 2003), pp. 251–67.

5 Robert Fossier, *La Terre et les hommes en Picardie jusqu'à la fin du XIIIe siècle* (Paris-Louvain, 1968).

6 Céline Perol, 'Le mariage et les lois sumptuaires en Toscane au XIVe siècle', in Josianne Teyssot (ed.), *Le Mariage au Moyen Age XIe–XVe siècle* (University of Clermont-Ferrand II, 1997), pp. 87–93.

Chapter 6 Money and the Nascent States

1 Cary J. Nederman, 'The Virtues of Necessity: Labor, Money and Corruption in John of Salisbury's Thought', *Viator* 33 (2002): 54–68.

2 Etienne Fournial, *Histoire monétaire de l'Occident médiéval* (Paris: Armand Colin, 1970), pp. 82–3.

3 Ferdinand Lot and Robert Fawtier, *Le Premier Budget de la monarchie française. Le compte général de 1202–1203* (Paris: Champion, 1932).

4 João Bernardo, *Poder e Dinheiro. Do Poder Pessoal ao Estado Impessoal no Regime Senhorial. Seculos V–XV*, 3 vols (Porto: ed. Afrontamento, 1995–2002). I am grateful to Maer Taveira for bringing this book to my attention and analysing it for me.

Chapter 7 Lending, Debt and Usury

1 See Giacomo Todeschini, 'La ricchezza degli Ebrei. Merci e denaro nella riflessione ebraica e nella definizione cristiana dell'usura alla fine del medioevo', in *Biblioteca degli Studi medievali* 15 (Centro italiano di studi sull'alto medioevo: Spoleto, 1989).

2 Jean Ibanès, *La Doctrine de l'Eglise et les réalités économiques au XIIIe siècle* (Paris: Presses Universitaires de France, 1967).

3 Thomas Aquinas, *Summa Theologica*, IIa–IIae, q. 77. art. 4, ad secundum.

4 Bibliothèque nationale, Paris, *Ms latin* 13472, fol. 3vb.
5 It was only from the sixteenth century that marriage, including the essential element of the consent of the spouses, was celebrated inside the church.
6 Jacques Le Goff, *Héros du Moyen Age: le saint et le roi* (Paris: Gallimard, Quarto, 2004) (first appeared in English in *Odysseus: Man in History-Anthropology-History Today* (Moscow: 1991), pp. 25–47).
7 Jacques Le Goff, *La Naissance du Purgatoire* (Paris: Gallimard, 1981), trans. Arthur Goldhammer as *The Birth of Purgatory* (Chicago: University of Chicago Press, 1984).
8 Nicole Bériou, 'L'esprit de lucre entre vice et vertu: variations sur l'amour de l'argent dans la prédication du XIIIe siècle', in *L'Argent au Moyen Age* (Paris: Publications de la Sorbonne, 1998), pp. 267–87.
9 Alain Guerreau, 'L'Europe médiévale: une civilisation sans la notion de risque', in *Risques. Les Cahiers de l'assurance* 31 (1997): 11–18. See also Pierre Toubert, 'La perception sociale du risque dans le monde méditerranéen au Moyen Age. Quelques observations préliminaires', in *Les Sociétés méditerranéennes face au risque: Disciplines, temps, espaces*, ed. Gérard Chastagnaret (Cairo: Institut français d'archéologie orientale, 2008), pp. 91–110; Sylvain Piron, 'L'apparition de *resicum* en Méditerranée occidentale aux XIIe–XIIIe siècles', in *Pour une histoire culturelle du risque. Genèse, évolution, actualité du concept dans les sociétés occidentales* (Strasbourg: Ed. Histoire et Anthropologie, 2004), pp. 59–76.
10 Ian P. Wei, 'Intellectuals and Money: Parisian Disputations about Annuities in the Thirteenth Century', *Bulletin of the John Rylands University Library of Manchester*, 83(3) (2001): 71–94.

Chapter 8 A New Wealth and a New Poverty

1 Lester K. Little, *Religious Poverty and the Profit Economy in Medieval Europe* (London: Paul Elek, 1978).
2 The great twentieth-century historian of medieval poverty was Michel Mollat. The papers given at his seminar were published under his direction in *Etudes sur l'histoire de la pauvreté* (Paris: Publications de la Sorbonne, 1974). See also his own remarkable synthesis: *The Poor in the Middle Ages* [1978], trans. Arthur Goldhammer (New Haven: Yale University Press, 1986).
3 I discuss the relationship between the mendicant orders and money in chapter 13.

4 For Peter John Olivi, see Alain Boureau and Sylvain Piron (eds), *Pierre de Jean Olivi, pensée scolastique, dissidence spirituelle et société* (Paris: Vrin, 2000). See also the translation of the *De contractibus* by Sylvain Piron, and, also by Sylvain Piron, 'Marchands et confesseurs, le *Traité des contrats* d'Olivi dans son context (Narbonne fin XIIIe–début du XIVe siècle)' in *L'Argent au Moyen Age* (Paris: Publications de la Sorbonne, 1998), pp. 289–308.
5 *Il 'Liber contractuum' dei Frati Minori di Padova e di Vicenza (1263–1302)*, ed. E. Bonato (Rome: Viella, 2002). See also André Vauchez, 'Francescanesimo veneto. A proposito del "Liber contractuum"', *Il Santo* (2003): 665–70.
6 See chapter 15 below.
7 In the *commenda* pure and simple, a sleeping partner lent an itinerant merchant the capital necessary for a trading voyage. If there was a loss, the lender bore the whole financial weight, the borrower losing only the value of his labour. If there was a profit, the lender who had remained at home was reimbursed and received a share in the profit, usually three quarters. In the *commenda* with the more specific name of *societas* or *collegantia*, the sleeping partner who stayed at home advanced two thirds of the capital while the borrower contributed one third and his labour. If there was a loss, it was shared in proportion to the capital invested. If there was profit, it was divided in half. This contract was generally agreed for one voyage. It might specify the nature and the destination of the enterprise as well as certain conditions, for example the currency in which the profit would be paid; or it might leave the borrower with complete freedom – the latter tending over time to become more independent. Here is the text of one such contract made in Genoa:

> Witnesses: Simone Bucuccio, Ogerio, Peloso, Ribaldo di Sauro and Genoardo Tosca. Stabile and Ansaldo Garraton have formed a *societas* in which, according to their statements, Stabile has contributed 88 lira and Ansaldo 44 lira. Ansaldo takes this capital to make it yield a profit, in Tunis or wherever else the vessel he joins might go, that is, the vessel of Baldizzone Grasso and Girardo. On his return he will repay the profit to Stabile or to his representative for the share out. After deducting the capital, they will divide the profits in half. Made in the Chapterhouse, 29 September.

Stabile also authorized Ansaldo to send this money to Genoa by whatever ship he chose.

8 We are well informed about these lending and credit activities, especially among the 'bankers' called Lombards, thanks to the research and publications of the Centro studi sui Lombardi e sul credito nel medioevo, established at Asti in the late twentieth century. See in particular: *Credito e società: le fonti, le tecniche e gli uomini, secc. XIV–XVI* (2000); *Politiche del credito. Investimento, consumo, solidarietà* (2004); *Prestito, credito, finanza in età basso-medievale* (2007). The centre was for a long time directed by Renato Bordone, professor at the University of Turin, who himself published important work on the activities of the Lombards. The phenomenon of indebtedness came to be of such importance that French royal justice created a crime punishable by imprisonment in the Châtelet prison for debts entered into in Paris. The penalization of debt became very important at the end of the Middle Ages and spread beyond the kingdom of France. It is discussed in a collective work dealing with France, Italy, Spain, England and the Empire from the thirteenth to the fifteenth century: *La Dette et le Juge*, ed. Julie Claustre (Paris: Publications de la Sorbonne, 2006).

9 See chapter 10.

Chapter 9 From the Thirteenth to the Fourteenth Century: Money in Crisis

1 Cary J. Nederman, 'The Virtues of Necessity: Labor, Money and Corruption in John of Salisbury's Thought', *Viator* 33 (2002): 54–68, esp. p. 86.

2 Robert-Henri Bautier, 'Le marchand lombard en France aux XIIIe et XIVe siècles', in *Le Marchand au Moyen Age* (XIXe congrès SHMES de Reims, 1988) (Paris: Publications de la Sorbonne, 1992), pp. 63–80.

3 David Kusman, 'Jean de Mirabello, dit Van Haelen. Haute finance et Lombards en Brabant dans le premier tiers du XIVe siècle', *Revue belge de philologie et d'histoire* 77(4) (1999): 843–931.

4 Renato Bordone and Franco Spinelli (eds), *Lombardi in Europa nel Medioevo* (Milan: 2005); Renato Bordone (ed.), *Dal banco di pegno all'alta finanza: Lombardi e mercanti-banchieri fra Paesi Bassi e Inghilterra nel Trecento*, Quaderni/Cahiers del Centro studi sui Lombardi, sul credito e sulla banca, 2 (2007–II).

5 Jaques Labrot, *Affairistes et usuriers au Moyen Age*, vol. 1: *Les Lombards, l'hérésie et l'Eglise* (Cahors: Ed. La Louve, 2008).

6 Raymond Cazelles, 'Quelques reflexions à propos des mutations de la monnaie royale française (1295–1360)', *Le Moyen Age* (1966): 83–105, 251–78.

7 From 1337, the mutations of silver coins were defined by the *pied de monnaie*, a formula which took into account the *prix* (official value of the coin in money of account), *taille* (number of coins minted from a mark) and *titre* (alloy or silver content of the coin), which made it possible to know the degree of weakening or strengthening involved. The higher the *pied*, the worse the money, that is, the less fine metal it contained. For a definition of the complicated but important notion of *pied de monnaie*, see Etienne Fournial, *Histoire monétaire de l'Occident médiéval* (Paris: 1970) pp. 30, 31; also John Bell Henneman, *Royal Taxation in Fourteenth Century France* (Princeton, NJ: Princeton University Press, 1971), appendix 1.

8 'The moneychangers will get, for each gold mark, 60 of these francs, and for each silver mark at the alloy of 4 deniers 12 grains, 108 sous tournois, and of all the other silver marks at the alloy of 4 deniers 12 grains, 4 livres 18 sous tournois, and the deniers of fine gold *au royal* which his Majesty or others on his behalf have struck will circulate only for 13 sous 4 deniers parisis each, since the publication of our ordinances on this subject; and the blancs deniers which circulated for 10 deniers tournois, which are *à la couronne* will circulate only for 4 deniers tournois each, and all other coins of gold or silver will be *mises au marc* for billon.' F. de Saulcy, *Recueil de documents relatifs à l'histoire des monnaies frappes par les rois de France*, vol. 1 (Paris: 1879), p. 455; modernized text in Fournial, *Histoire monétaire de l'Occident medieval*, p. 158.

9 Ugo Tucci, 'Alla origini dello spirito capitalistico a Venezia: la previsione economica', in *Studi in onore di Amintore Fanfani*, vol. 3, ed. A. Giuffre (Milan: Giuffrè, 1962). As will later become clear, I have used the work of Tucci on the existence of an anticipatory mentality in medieval Venice, but without accepting his hypothesis that this is an early sign of the capitalist mentality.

Chapter 10 The Perfecting of the Financial System at the End of the Middle Ages

1 I reproduce here text taken from my book of 1956: *Marchands et banquiers du Moyen Age* (Paris: Presses Universitaires de France, 1956), pp. 30–2.

2 *Marchands et banquiers*, p. 27.

3 Medieval accounting had its own great historian, Federico Melis, author of *Storia della ragioneria* (Bologna: C. Buffi, 1950). Melis constructed in Prato, round the archives of the great Tuscan merchant Francesco di Marco Datini, a fine centre for the study of medieval accounting and, more generally, of the economy.
4 Giulia Scarcia, *Lombardi oltralpe nel Trecento. Il 'Registrum' 9, I dell'Archivio di Stati di Friburgo*, Pisa, ETS, Piccola Biblioteca Gisem 19 (2001).
5 Beatrice Del Bo, 'Elite bancaria a Milano a metà Quattrocento: prime note', *Quaderni del Centro di Studi sui Lombardi, sul credito e sulla banca* 1 (2007): 173.
6 But they are very different from the modern societies with a personality independent of their members.
7 Michel Mollat, *Jacques Coeur ou l'esprit d'entreprise* (Paris: Aubier, 1988).

Chapter 11 Towns, States and Money at the End of the Middle Ages

1 Jean-Luc Pinol, *Histoire de l'Europe urbaine*, vol. 1 (Paris: Seuil, 2003), p. 575.
2 F. Humbert, 'Les finances municipales de la ville de Dijon au milieu du XIVe siècle à 1477' (Paris: 1961); Henri Dubois, 'Les fermes du vingtième à Dijon à la fin du XIe siècle. Fiscalité Economie Société', in *L'Argent au Moyen Age*, Colloque of 1997 (Paris: Publications de la Sorbonne, 1998), pp. 159–71.
3 The value of all their possessions.
4 Pierre Monnet, 'Le financement de l'indépendance urbaine par les élites argentées', in *L'Argent au Moyen Age*, pp. 187–207.
5 Marc Boone, 'Stratégies fiscales et financières des élites urbaines et de l'Etat bourguignon naissant dans l'ancien comté de Flandre (XIVe–XVIe siècle)', in *L'Argent au Moyen Age*, pp. 235–53.
6 Bernard Guillemain, *La Cour pontifical d'Avignon 1309–1376. Etude d'une société* (Paris: De Boccard, 1962); Jean Favier, *Les Finances pontificales à l'époque du grand schisme d'Occident, 1378–1409* (Paris: 1966); Jean Favier, *Les Papes d'Avignon* (Paris: De Boccard, 2006); which should be supplemented by Yves Renouard, *Les Relations des papes d'Avignon et des compagnies commerciales et bancaires de 1316 à 1378* (Paris: De Boccard, 1941).
7 Ferdinand Lot and Robert Fawtier, *Histoire des institutions françaises au Moyen Age*, vol. 2: *Institutions royales*, p. 279.

Chapter 12 Prices, Wages and Coin in the Fourteenth and Fifteenth Centuries

1 Jérôme Baschet, *La Civilisation féodale. De l'an mil à la colonisation de l'Amérique* (Paris: Aubier, 2004), pp. 228–78.
2 I draw here mainly on the work of Philippe Contamine, Marc Bompaire, Stéphane Lebecq and Jean-Luc Sarrazin, *L'Economie medievale*, 3rd edn (Paris: Armand Colin, 2003).
3 Julien Demade, 'Transactions foncières et transactions frumentaires: une relation de contrainte ou d'opportunité? L'exemple des tenanciers de l'hôpital de Nuremberg (1432–1527)', in Laurent Feller and Chris Wickham (eds), *Le Marché de la terre au Moyen Age* (Ecole française de Rome, 2005), pp. 341–403.
4 Marian Malowist, 'The Problem of the Inequality of Economic Development in Europe in the Later Middle Ages', *Economic History Review*, second ser., 29(1) (1966): 15–28.
5 Laurent Feller, *Paysans et seigneurs au Moyen Age, VIIIe–XVe siècles* (Paris: Armand Colin, 2007).
6 Douglas Knoop and G. P. Jones, *The Medieval Mason* (Manchester: Manchester University Press, 1933).
7 There is an exemplary study of these problems in Céline Perol, 'Le mariage et les lois sumptuaires en Toscane au XIVe siècle', in Josianne Teyssot (ed.), *Le Mariage au Moyen Age XIe–XVe siècle* (University of Clermont-Ferrand II, 1997), pp. 87–93. For luxury in foodstuffs, see Antonella Campanelli, 'La table sous contrôle. Les banquets et l'excès alimentaire dans le cadre des lois somptuaires en Italie entre le Moyen Age et la Renaissance', *Food and History* 4(2) (2006, appeared in 2007): 131–50.
8 Jean Meuvret, 'Circulation monétaire et utilisation économique de la monnaie dans la France aux XVIe et XVIIe siècle', in *Etudes d'histoire moderne et contemporaine* 1 (1947), reprinted in *Etudes d'histoire économique, Cahiers des Annales* XXXII (Paris, 1971), pp. 127ff.
9 This is perhaps as a result of English precocity in financial matters, and the ambiguity of the term 'money', analogous to that of the Italian *pecunia*, inherited from Antiquity.
10 Alain Guerreau, 'Avant le marché, les marchés: en Europe, XIIIe–XVIIIe siècle', in Laurent Feller and Chris Wickham (eds), *Le Marché de la terre au Moyen Age* (Ecole française de Rome, 2005).
11 This is argued by François Menant in Feller and Wickham, *Le Marché de la terre au Moyen Age*, p. 211.

12 Barbara H. Rosenwein, *To Be the Neighbour of Saint Peter: The Social Meaning of Cluny's Property, 909–1049* (Ithaca-London: Cornell University Press, 1989).
13 Dominique Barthélemy, *La Société dans le comté de Vendôme de l'an mil au XIVe siècle* (Paris: Fayard, 1993).

Chapter 13 The Mendicant Orders and Money

1 Of the many works of Giacomo Todeschini, apart from the one I regard as most valuable, *I Mercanti e il Tempio. La società cristiana e il circulo virtuoso della ricchezza fra Medioevo ed età moderno* (Bologna, 2002), the one which most clearly articulates this interpretation of the role of the Franciscans in the development of an economic theory which would later, if oriented towards the collective good, be the capitalist theory based on the wise use of wealth, was *Ricchezza francescana. Dalla povertà volontaria alla società di mercato* (Bologna: il Mulino, 2004), translated as *Franciscan Wealth: from Voluntary Poverty to Market Society* (New York: Franciscan Institute, St Bonaventure University, 2009). The distinguished historian from the University of Bologna, Paolo Prodi, has also argued for, even taken further, the idea of the birth in the Middle Ages of an economic power distinct from political power: see his *Settimano non rubare. Furto e mercato nella storia dell'Occidente* (Bologna: il Mulino, 2009) (the title referring to the Seventh Commandment).
2 'Monts-de-piété', in André Vauchez (ed.), *Dictionnaire encyclopédique du Moyen Age* (Paris: Le Cerf, 1997).
3 Nicole Bériou and Jacques Chiffoleau (eds), *Economie et religion: l'expérience des ordres mendiants (XIIIe–XVe siècle)* (Lyon: Presses Universitaires de Lyon, 2009).
4 'Les comptabilités pontificales' in *Mélanges de l'Ecole française de Rome, Moyen Age* (2006): 165–268.
5 N. Coquery, F. Menant and F. Weber, *Ecrire, compter, mesurer. Vers une histoire des rationalités practiques* (Paris, 2006).

Chapter 14 Humanism, Patronage and Money

1 André Vauchez, '*Homo mercator vix aut numquam potest Deo placere*: quelques réflexions sur l'attitude des milieux ecclésiastiques face aux nouvelles formes de l'activité économique au XIIe et au début du XIIIe siècle', in *Le Marchand au Moyen Age* (Paris: SHMES, 1992), pp. 211–17. Nevertheless, it should be noted that the introduction – all that survives – to the Bull of canonization

emphasizes that St Homobonus was canonized *in spite of* having been a merchant.

2 Nicole Bériou, 'L'esprit de lucre entre vice et vertu', in *L'Argent au Moyen Age*, Colloque of 1997 (Paris: Publications de la Sorbonne, 1998), pp. 267–87.

3 Patrick Gilli, 'La place de l'argent dans la pensée humaniste italienne au XVe siècle', in *L'Argent au Moyen Age*, pp. 309–26; Daniel R. Lesnick, 'Dominican Preaching and the Creation of Capitalist Ideology in Late-Medieval Florence', in *Memorie Domenicane* 8–9 (1977–8): 199–247. In most of the texts cited here, which were increasingly, with the passage of time, written in the vernacular, not Latin, the word usually employed for 'money' is *denaio* in Italian. This refers to the denier, and we see from the vocabulary that we have not yet reached the age when, to indicate the monetary form of wealth, people spoke of 'money'.

4 Rinaldo Comba, 'La législation somptuaire d'Amédée VIII', in *Amédée VIII–Felix V, premier duc de Savoie et pape (1383–1451)*, Colloque international, Ripaille-Lausanne, 1990, ed. B. Andenmatten and Agostino Paravicini Bagliani (Lausanne, 1992), pp. 191–200.

5 The word used is *denari*, the word most frequently used where we would speak of money. I would like to thank my friend Christiane Klapisch-Zuber for drawing this interesting anecdote to my attention.

Chapter 15 Capitalism or *Caritas*?

1 Philippe Norel, *L'Histoire économique globale* (Paris: Seuil, 2009).

2 Anita Guerreau-Jalabert, '*Spiritus* et *caritas*. Le baptême dans la société médiévale', in F. Héritier-Augé and E. Copet-Rougier (eds), *La Parenté spirituelle* (Paris: Ed. des Archives contemporaines, 1995), pp. 133–203; Anita Guerreau-Jalabert, '*Caritas* y don en la sociedad medieval occidental', *Hispania. Revista Espanola de historia*, 60/1/204 (2000): 27–62.

3 See Hélène Pétré, *Caritas. Etude sur le vocabulaire latin de la charité chrétienne* (Louvain: 1948).

4 Jacques Chiffoleau, *La Comptabilité de l'au-delà. Les hommes, la mort et la religion dans la région d'Avignon à la fin du Moyen Age (vers 1320–vers 1408)* (Ecole française de Rome, 1980).

5 Alain Guerreau, 'Avant le marché, les marchés: en Europe, XIIIe–XVIIIe siècles, notes critiques', *Annales ESC* (2001): 1129–75.

6 *Dictionnaire culturel* (Le Robert, 2005), vol. 1, p. 1056.
7 Jacques Le Goff, *Un long Moyen Age* (Paris: Tallandier, 2004).
8 Bartolomé Clavero, *Antidora. Antropologia católica de la economia moderna* (Milan: Giuffre, 1991), trans. French as *La Grâce du don. Anthropologie catholique de l'économie moderne*, with a preface by Jacques Le Goff (Paris: Albin Michel, 1996).
9 Philippe Norel, *L'Invention du marché. Une histoire économique de la mondialisation* (Paris: Seuil, 2004). In a later book (*L'Histoire économique globale* (Paris: Seuil, 2009), which I have already used for the definitions of capitalism, Norel thought he could detect the first forms of capitalism in the form of an agrarian capitalism in sixteenth-century England, which would be the basis of the industrialization by which capitalism spread in the eighteenth century, when what Marx called the 'primitive accumulation of capital' began to appear.

Conclusion

1 Karl Polanyi and Conrad M. Arensberg (eds), *Trade and Market in the Early Empires* (New York: Free Press, 1956).
2 Paolo Prodi, *Settimo non rubare. Furto e mercato nella storia dell'Occidente* (Bologna: 2009).

Bibliography

I give here, in addition to works cited in the text, those I have drawn on directly in writing this book.

Abel, W., *Massenarmut und Hungerkrisen im vorindustriellen Deutschland* (Göttingen: Vandenhoeck & Ruprecht, 1972).

Angholm, O., *Economics in the Medieval Schools: Wealth, Exchange, Value, Money and Usury According to the Paris Theological Tradition 1200–1350* (Leiden: E. J. Brill, 1992).

Archéologie des villages désertés: Dracy (Paris: Armand Colin, 1970).

L'Argent au Moyen Age, Colloque of 1997 (Paris: Publications de la Sorbonne, 1998).

Bailly-Maître, Marie-Christine, *L'Argent. Du minerai au pouvoir dans la France médiévale* (Paris: Ed. Picard, 2002).

Baschet, Jérôme, *La Civilisation féodale. De l'an mil à la colonisation de l'Amérique* (Paris: Aubier, 2004).

Belaubre, J. and Collin, B., *Les Monnaies de France. Histoire d'un people* (Paris: Perrin, 1992).

Bériou, Nicole, 'L'esprit de lucre entre vice et vertu: variations sur l'amour de l'argent dans la prédication du XIIIe siècle', in *L'Argent au Moyen Age*, pp. 267–87.

Bériou, Nicole and Chiffoleau, Jacques, *Economie et religion. L'expérience des ordres mendiants (XIIIe–XVe siècles)* (Lyon: P. U. de Lyon, 2009).

Bernardo, João, *Poder e Dinheiro. Do Poder Pessoal ao Estado Impessoal no Regime Senhorial. Seculos V–XV*, ed. Afrontamento, 3 vols (1995–2002).

Beveridge, W., *Prices and Wages in England from the Twelfth to the Nineteenth Century* (London: Longman Green, 1939).

Bisson, Thomas M., *Conservation of Coinage: Monetary Exploitation and its Restraint in France, Catalonia and Aragon (c. AD 1000–c. 1225)* (Oxford: Clarendon, 1979).

Bloch, Marc, 'Le problem de l'or au Moyen Age', *Annales d'histoire économique et sociale* 5 (1933): 1–34.

Bloch, Marc, 'Economie–nature ou économie–argent, un faux dilemme', *Annales d'histoire sociale* (1939), vol. 1, pp. 7–16.

Bloch, Marc, *Esquisse d'une histoire monétaire de l'Europe* (Paris: Librairie Armand Colin, 1954).

Bompaire, Marc and Dumas, F., *Numismatique médiévale* (Turnhout: Brepols, 2000).

Bordone, Renato and Spinelli, Franco (eds), *Lombardi in Europa nel Medioevo* (Milan: F. Angeli, 2005).

Boschieri, G. and Molina, B., *Politiche del credito. Investimento, consumo, solidarietà* (Asti 2004).

Boureau, Alain and Piron, Sylvain (eds), *Pierre de Jean Olivi, pensée scolastique, dissidence spirituelle et société* (Paris: Vrin, 2000).

Bourin, Monique and Martinez Sopena, P. (eds), *Pour une anthropologie du prélèvement seigneurial dans les campagnes de l'Occident médiéval. Les mots, les temps, les lieux* (Paris: Publications de la Sorbonne, 2007).

Braudel, F., *Civilisation matérielle et capitalisme (XVe–XVIIIe siècle)* (Paris: Armand Colin, 1979).

Braunstein, Philippe, *Travail et entreprise au Moyen Age* (Brussels: De Boeck, 2003).

Bridrey, E., *La Théorie de la monnaie au XIVe siècle, Nicolas Oresme* (Caen 1906).

Britnell, R. H., *The Commercialisation of English Society (1000–1500)* (Cambridge: Cambridge University Press, 1993).

Brown, E., *Customary Aids and Royal Finance in Capetian France. The Marriage Aid of Philip the Fair* (Cambridge, MA: Medieval Academy of America, 1992).

Chiffoleau, Jacques, *La Comptabilité de l'au-delà. Les hommes, la mort et la religion dans la région d'Avignon à la fin du Moyen Age (vers 1320–vers 1408)* (Rome: Ecole française de Rome, 1980).

Cipolla, C. M., *Money, Prices and Civilization in the Mediterranean World: Fifth to Seventeenth Centuries* (Princeton: Princeton University Press, 1956).

Claustre, J. (ed.), *La Dette et le Juge. Juridiction gracieuse et juridiction contentieuse du XIIIe au XVe siècle* (Paris: Publications de la Sorbonne, 2002).

Clavero, Bartolomé, *Antidora. Antropologia católica de la economia moderna* (Milan: Giuffre, 1991), trans. French as *La Grâce du don.*

Anthropologie catholique de l'économie moderne (Paris: Albert Michael, 1996).

Contamine, Philippe, Bompaire, Marc, Lebecq, Stéphane and Sarrazin, Jean-Luc, *L'Economie médiévale*, 3rd edn (Paris: Armand Colin, 2003).

The Dawn of Modern Banking, Center for Medieval and Renaissance Studies (New Haven–London: Yale University Press, 1979).

Day, J., 'The Great Bullion Famine of the Fifteenth Century', *Past and Present* 79 (May 1978): 3–54.

Day, J., *Etudes d'histoire monétaire* (Lille: Presses universitaires de Lille, 1986).

Day, J., *Monnaies et marchés au Moyen Age* (Paris: Comité pour l'Histoire Economique et Financière, 1994).

Del Bo, Beatrice, 'Elite bancaria a Milano a metà Quattrocento: prime note', in *Quaderni del Centro di Studi sui Lombardi, sul credito e sulla banca* 1 (2007).

Demade, Julian, 'Ponction féodale et société rurale en Allemagne du Sud (XIe–XVIe siècle). Essai sur la fonction des transactions monétaires dans les économies non capitalistes', thesis, Marc Bloch University, Strasbourg II, 2004.

De Roover, Raymond, *Money, Banking and Credit in Mediaeval Bruges* (Cambridge, MA: Mediaeval Academy of America, 1948).

De Roover, Raymond, *L'Evolution de la lettre de change* (Paris: Armand Colin, 1953).

De Roover, Raymond, *The Rise and Decline of the Medici Bank (1397–1494)* (Cambridge, MA: Harvard University Press, 1963).

Duplessy, J., 'La circulation des monnaies arabes en Europe occidentale du VIIIe au XIIIe siècle', *Revue numismatique* 18 (1956): 101–64.

Favier, Jean, *Les Finances pontificales à l'époque du grand schism d'Occident, 1378–1409* (Paris: E. de Boccard, 1966).

Favier, Jean, *De l'or et des épices. Naissance de l'homme d'affaires au Moyen Age* (Paris: Fayard, 1987).

Feller, Laurent and Wickham, Chris (eds), *Le Marché de la terre au Moyen Age* (Rome: Ecole française de Rome, 2005).

Fossier, Robert, *La Terre et les hommes en Picardie jusqu'à la fin du XIIIe siècle* (Paris-Louvain, 1968).

Fossier, Robert, *Histoire sociale de l'Occident médiéval* (Paris: Armand Colin, 1970).

Fossier, Robert, *La société médiévale* (Paris: Armand Colin, 1991).

Fourquin, Guy, *Histoire économique de l'Occident médiéval* (Paris-Louvain: Beatrice-Nauwelaerts and Nauwelaerts, 1969).

Frugoni, Chiara, *L'Affare migliore di Enrico: Giotto e la cappella Scrovegni* (Turin: Einaudi, 2008).

Geremek, Bronislaw, *Le Salariat dans l'artisanat parisien aux XIIe–XVe siècles* (Paris: Editions de l'Ecole des Hautes Etudes en Sciences, 1969).

Graus, Frantisek, 'La crise monétaire du XIVe siècle', *Revue belge de philologie et d'histoire* 29 (1951): 445–54.

Grierson, Philip, *Monnaies du Moyen Age* (Fribourg: Office du livre, 1976).

Guerreau, Alain, 'Avant le marché, les marchés: en Europe, XIIIe–XVIIIe siècle, notes critiques', *Annales ESC* (2001): 1129–75.

Guerreau-Jalabert, Anita, '*Spiritus* et *caritas*. Le baptême dans la société médiévale', in F. Héritier-Augé and E. Copet-Rougier (eds), *La Parenté spirituelle* (Paris: Ed. des Archives contemporaines, 1995), pp. 133–203.

Guerreau-Jalabert, Anita, '*Caritas* y don en la sociedad medieval occidental', *Hispania. Revista Espanola de historia*, 60/1/204 (2000): 27–62.

Ibanès, Jean, *La Doctrine de l'Eglise et les réalités économiques au XIIIe siècle* (Paris: PUF, 1967).

Jensen, J. S. (ed.), *Coinage and Monetary Circulation in the Baltic Area* (Copenhagen: NNA, 1981).

Lane, F. C. and Müller, R., *Money and Banking in Mediaeval and Renaissance Venice*, vol. 1 (Baltimore: Johns Hopkins Press, 1985).

La Roncière, Charles de, *Un changeur florentin du Trecento: Lipo di Fede del Sega (vers 1285–vers 1363)* (Paris: SEVPEN, 1973).

La Roncière, Charles de, *Prix et salaires à Florence au XIVe siècle 1280–1380* (Rome: Ecole française de Rome, 1982).

Le Goff, Jacques, *Marchands et banquiers du Moyen Age* (Paris: Presses Universitaires de France, 1956).

Le Goff, Jacques, *La Bourse et la Vie. Economie et religion au Moyen Age* (Paris 1986), trans. Patricia Ranum as *Your Money or Your Life. Economy and Religion in the Middle Ages* (New York: Zone Books, 1988).

Little, Lester K., *Religious Poverty and the Profit Economy in Medieval Europe* (London: Paul Elek, 1978).

Lombard, M., 'Les bases monétaires d'une suprématie économique: l'or musulman du VIIe au XIe siècle', *Annales ESC* (1947): 143–60.

Lopez, Robert S., 'Settecento anni fà: il ritorno all'oro nell'Occidente duecentesco', *Rivista storico italiana* 65 (1952): 19–55, 161–98.

Lot, Ferdinand and Fawtier, Robert, *Le Premier Budget de la monarchie française. Le compte général de 1202–1203* (Paris: Champion, 1932).

Melis, Federico, *Storia della ragioneria* (Bologna: C. Buffi, 1950).

Miskimin, H. A., *Money, Prices and Foreign Exchange in Fourteenth Century France* (New Haven: Yale University Press, 1963).
Miyamatsu, H., *La Naissance du riche* (Mercuès: Les Perséides, 2006).
Mollat, Michel, 'Usure et hérésie: les "Cahorsins" chez eux', in *Studi in memoria di Federico Melis* (Naples 1978), vol. 1, pp. 269–78.
Mollat, Michel, *Les Pauvres au Moyen Age* (Paris: 1978), trans. Arthur Goldhammer as *The Poor in the Middle Ages* (New Haven: Yale University Press, 1986).
Murray, Alexander, *Reason and Society in the Middle Ages* (Oxford: Oxford University Press, 1978).
Nahon, G., 'Le credit et les Juifs dans la France du XIIIe siècle', *Annales ESC* (1969): 1121–44.
Norel, Philippe, *L'Invention du marché. Une histoire économique de la mondialisation* (Paris: Seuil, 2004).
Norel, Philippe, *L'Histoire économique globale* (Paris: Seuil, 2009).
L'Or au Moyen Age, colloque du CUER-MA, (Marseille: Diffusion, J. Lafitte, 1983).
Oresme, Nicole, *De moneta*, trans. into English by Charles Johnson (London: Nelson and Sons, 1956).
Otaka, Y., 'La valeur monétaire d'après les oeuvre arthuriennes', in *Temps et histoire dans le roman arthurien*, ed. J.-C. Faucon (Toulouse: Editions universitaires du Sud, 1999).
Polanyi, Karl and Arensberg, Conrad M. (eds), *Trade and Market in the Early Empires* (New York: Free Press, 1956).
Postan, M. M., 'The Rise of a Money Economy', *Economic History Review* 17 (1944): 123–34.
Postan, M. M. (ed.), *The Cambridge Economic History of Europe*, vol. 2: *Trade and Industry in the Middle Ages* (Cambridge: Cambridge University Press, 1952); vol. 3: *Economic Organisation and Policies in the Middle Ages* (Cambridge: Cambridge University Press, 1963).
Renouard, Yves, *Les Relations des papes d'Avignon et des compagnies commerciales et bancaires de 1316 à 1378* (Paris: E. de Boccard, 1941).
Renouard, Yves, *Les Hommes d'affaires italiens du Moyen Age* (Paris: A. Colin, 1949).
Rey, M., *Les Finances royales sous Charles VI. Les causes du déficit* (Paris: Imprimerie nationale, 1965).
Sapori, Armando, *Le Marchand Italien au Moyen Age* (Paris: SEVPEN, 1952).
Schmitt, J.-C., 'L'Eglise médiévale et l'argent', *Journal des Caisses d'épargne* 3 (May–June 1986).

Spufford, Peter, *Money and its Use in Medieval Europe* (Cambridge: Cambridge University Press, 1988).

Suchodolski, Stanislaw, 'Les débuts du monnayage en Pologne', *Revue Suisse de numismatique* 51 (1972): 131–5.

Tits-Dieuaide, M. J., *La Formation des prix céréaliers en Brabant et en Flandre au XVe siècle* (Brussels: Editions de l'Université de Bruxelles, 1975).

Todeschini, Giacomo, *I Mercanti e il Tempio. La società cristiana e il circulo virtuoso della ricchezza fra Medioevo ed età moderno* (Bologna: Il Mulino, 2002).

Todeschini, Giacomo, *Ricchezza francescana. Dalla povertà volontaria alla società di mercato* (Bologna: il Mulino, 2004), trans. as *Franciscan Wealth: From Voluntary Poverty to Market Society* (New York: Franciscan Institute, St Bonaventure University, 2009).

Wei, I. P., 'Intellectuals and Money: Parisian Disputations about Annuities in the Thirteenth Century', *Bulletin of the John Rylands University Library of Manchester* 83(3) (2001): 71–94.

Wolff, P., *Automne du Moyen Age ou printemps des temps nouveaux? L'économie européenne aux XIVe et XVe siècles* (Paris: Aubier, 1986).

Index